RAIL INDUSTRY LIABILITIES

By

Dan Mitchell, John Morrell and Rupert Nevin

RAIL INDUSTRY LIABILITIES
By
Dan Mitchell, John Morrell and Rupert Nevin

ISBN: 978-0-9565037-01

Published by DWF LLP
in conjunction with Writersworld Ltd.

Copy Edited by Brian Stanton

Cover Design by Charles Leveroni

Printed and bound by
www.printondemand-worldwide.com

www.writersworld.co.uk
Writersworld, 2 Bear Close Flats, Bear Close, Woodstock,
Oxfordshire, OX20 1JX, United Kingdom

About the Authors

Dan Mitchell is a Partner and head of the rail unit at DWF and has also has acted for over 10 years for train operating companies, BRB (Residuary) Limited and freight carriers in the defence of high value public liability and employers' liability claims.

John Morrell is a Director with DWF in their London office and has specialised in liability claims against local authorities for 30 years and has handled a number of leading cases which have dealt with the extent of the duty of care owed by local authorities in negligence.

Rupert Nevin is a Partner within the DWF Regulatory team in their Leeds office and has over twenty years experience acting for individuals and organisations within the transport sector being investigated, prosecuted or otherwise falling under the scrutiny of UK Government agencies and departments including Health and Safety Executive for regulatory crime, "white collar" criminal offences, corporate killing and other health and safety offences.

http://www.dwf.co.uk/

Preface

All claims and legal issues are governed by general principles. These are the subject of the many well-known textbooks which provide an excellent source of research and guidance. Increasingly, however, lawyers and claims' handlers find themselves specialising in particular sectors. It is because of this specialisation that we have written this book to deal with claims against, and the regulation of, the rail industry.

As will be seen in the book, the legal duties and liabilities of railway companies were first established during the 19th century when, of course, the railways were being established. However, not only has the common law developed, but statutory duties, and duties emanating from the European Union, have created new obligations on railway companies and other organisations, an example being the duty owed to trespassers. The common law relating to trespassers developed in cases brought against railway companies. Parliament then passed the Occupiers' Liability Act 1984 which created a statutory duty. Another area which is of particular concern to railway companies is its potential liability to former employees who now suffer from industrial disease, particularly arising out of contact with asbestos. The courts have handed down a number of important decisions in cases concerned with mesothelioma and pleural plaques. The impact of these has led to considerable pressure on Parliament to pass legislation to try to ensure that compensation reaches those who deserve it.

This book has been written not as a definitive textbook, but to give guidance to those who deal with legal issues relating to railway companies. We would like to thank all who have contributed, in particular Adrian Mansbridge, Helen Ellsworth and Ricky Lindsay and also to Clara Heylen and Sarah Pegram, who have provided secretarial and typing assistance.

Finally, this book represents the law as at March 2010.

CONTENTS

(References are to paragraph numbers)

LIST OF CASES

(References are to paragraph numbers)

LIST OF STATUTES

(References are to paragraph numbers)

LIST OF STATUTORY INSTRUMENTS

(References are to paragraph numbers)

ONE

INTRODUCTION TO THE LEGAL POSITION OF COMPANIES AND ORGANISATIONS OPERATING WITHIN THE RAILWAY INDUSTRY

Introduction

1.1   The history of the railway has involved individual railway companies, the nationalised railway system and, since privatisation, train operating companies and bodies responsible for the infrastructure. For ease of reference in this book, the term "Railway Company" is used to cover all those involved in operating and running the railways past and present.

1.2   This book considers legal issues arising out of the relationship between railway companies and their passengers, their employees, and other persons on the railway. In doing so, the starting point is the common law, both in terms of negligence and nuisance. Railway companies operate under statute and also owe statutory duties both to users of the railway and their employees. The duty owed to employees is, of course, governed by the common law. The common law duty was enhanced by statute over the years and the legal position is now increasingly covered by the Health and Safety at Work Act 1974 and the Regulations made under that Act.

Negligence

1.3   In order to establish negligence, it is necessary for a claimant to establish three requirements:

1

(i)   The defendant owed him a duty of care, the scope of which includes avoidance of the damage in fact suffered;

(ii)   The defendant was in breach of that duty;

(iii)   The claimant has suffered damage by reason of that breach.

1.4   The modern law of negligence, by which the courts decide whether a particular situation gives rise to a duty of care in law, can be traced back to *Donoghue v Stevenson*[1]. In that case, Lord Atkin formulated his famous 'neighbour' principle:

You must take reasonable care to avoid acts or omissions which you can reasonably foresee would be likely to injure a neighbour. Who, then, in law is my neighbour? The answer seems to be - persons who are so closely and directly affected by my act that I ought reasonably to have them in contemplation as being so affected when I am directing my mind to the acts or omissions that are called in question.

1.5   It should be noted that the duty of care in *Donoghue v Stevenson* is a duty to avoid acts or omissions that the defendant can reasonably foresee would be likely to cause personal injury or damage to the property of persons who are closely and directly affected by the defendant's conduct.

1.6   As far as railway companies are concerned, a claimant will always be in a position to establish the existence of a duty of care. While there used to be only a limited, if any, duty owed to trespassers, a duty of care was imposed in certain circumstances, following the House of Lords decision in *British Railways Board v Herrington*[2] and a duty of care is now set out in the Occupiers Liabilities Act 1984. It is not proposed here to analyse the many cases in which the courts

---

[1] [1932] AC 562

[2] [1972] 2 WL537

have explored the question whether or not a duty of care exists. As far as railway companies are concerned, cases involving negligence are concerned with breach of duty and damage.

1.7 Nuisance is an act or omission which interferes with a person's enjoyment of his ownership or occupation of land. Accordingly, there can be claims brought by railway companies against neighbouring landowners for nuisance; for example where a neighbouring landowner's tree falls on a railway line causing damage. The activities of railway companies can, of course, themselves give rise to nuisance, however, it must be remembered that railway companies operate under statute. If nuisance results from the performance of a statutory duty, there is no liability without negligence.[3]

Statutory duty

1.8 Actions for breach of statutory duty form a separate category of the common law, although actions for negligence and breach of statutory duty are often closely linked. While it is sometimes difficult to establish whether breach of a particular statutory duty gives rise to a claim for damages, in the areas specifically considered in this book, the position is normally reasonably clear. In particular, in cases involving employees, the regulations which are referred to in the chapter on Employer's Liability will mostly give rise to a claim for breach of statutory duty under the Health and Safety at Work Act 1974.

Human Rights Act 1998

1.9 The Human Rights Act 1998 came into force on 2 October

---

[3] *Department of Transport v North West Water* [1983] 1 All ER 892

2000. The Act incorporates the European Convention on Human Rights into UK law. Under S.6 of the Act, it is unlawful for a public authority to act in a way that is incompatible with the European Convention on Human Rights. Under S.6 (3)(b), a "public authority includes any person certain of whose functions are of a public nature". It is submitted that railway companies fall within this definition, and indeed, Railtrack plc was referred to specifically in guidance published by the Home Office before the Human Rights Act came into force. On the whole, however, it seems that existing remedies provided by common law or statute are adequate to deal with the relationship between railway companies and passengers and employees. As a result, there seems limited scope for influence from ideas contained in the European Convention on Human Rights.

The Relationship between different Rail Industry Parties

1.10 The privatisation of the Railways in 1994 brought with it the potential for claims between rail industry parties and the possibility of it becoming difficult for a member of the travelling public to identify the appropriate rail industry party against whom to present a claim. For this reason the Claims Allocation and Handling Agreement was drafted and entered into by all rail industry parties. This book seeks to provide an analysis of the key clauses of the Claims Allocation Handling Agreement and their practical implication when dealing with claims.

Health and Safety Regulation and Enforcement

1.11 The introduction of legislation which imposed duties on employers brought with it the possibility of claims being made for breach of statutory duty. Statutory regulation also introduced the possibility of criminal sanctions. The regulation of health and safety, both relating to employees and others on the railways is, following the Railways Act

4

1993, to be found principally in the Health and Safety at Work Act 1974, which provides for the possibility of criminal sanctions both against companies and individuals. More recently, the Corporate Manslaughter and Corporate Homicide Act 2007, introduced in part as a result of serious incidents occurring on the railways, has provided a new offence which can result in the imposition of substantial fines on companies and organisations involved in operating the railways. The Health and Safety Offences Act 2008 has increased the courts' sentencing powers in relation to health and safety offences.

1.12   As far as the railways are concerned, health and safety enforcement is the responsibility of the Office of Rail Regulation which oversees not only duties and responsibilities under the Health and Safety at Work Act 1974, but also other statutory duties such as those under the Railways and Other Guided Systems (Safety) Regulations 2006.

TWO

CLAIMS FOR INJURY AND LOSS ARISING OUT OF THE OPERATION OF RAILWAYS

Introduction

2.1   It is relevant to consider both the position arising at common law and also out of statute. Much of a railway company's activities arise under statute. A railway company may therefore escape liability for something which would otherwise give rise to a claim, if damage arises necessarily from the exercise of a power conferred by the statute, provided that such power is exercised without negligence. In *Department of Transport v North West Water*[4] Webster J said:

In the absence negligence, a body is not liable for a nuisance which is attributable to the exercise by it of a power conferred by statute if, by statute, it is neither expressly made liable, nor expressly exempted from liability, for nuisance.

Common Law

2.2   At common law, the position of a railway company is that of a carrier. The common law duty of a carrier was set out by the House of Lords in *Barkway v South Wales Transport Co Limited*[5] Lord Radcliffe said:

A carrier's obligation to his passengers, whether expressed

---

[4] [1983] 1 All ER 892
[5] [1950] 1 All ER 392

7

to be in contract or in tort, is to provide a carriage that is as free from defects as the exercise of all reasonable care can make it.

2.3   The duty of care owed by a carrier would appear to be the same as that owed in negligence, in the ordinary way, namely to take reasonable care in the circumstances to avoid acts or omissions which can reasonably be foreseen as likely to injure the person or property of others.

2.4   Because injury to passengers can be foreseen, there is no distinction to be drawn between the duty owed to passengers who have paid a fare, and those who are travelling with the benefit of a free pass. The duty is, for example, owed to a post office employee travelling with the post, and to a child carried free of charge. In *Austin v G.W. Railway*[6], the railway company was held liable for injury to a three year old child travelling with her mother, but without a ticket. Blackburn J said:

... the right which a passenger by railway has to be carried safely, does not depend on his having made a contract, but that the fact of his being a passenger casts a duty on the company to carry him safely.

2.5   A carrier is not liable for a latent defect which cannot reasonably be detected[7]. In *Redhead v Midland Railway* a carriage left the rails because of a defective wheel. There was no liability on the railway company because the defect was latent and could not be detected with reasonable care.

The Duty Owed to Passengers on Trains

2.6   A passenger injured whilst using the railway must prove a breach of the duty of care owed to him. In reality, however, many events occurring on the railway are likely to be subject

---

[6] (1867) LR 2QB 442
[7] [1869] LR 4 QB 379

to the doctrine of *res ipsa loquitur*, namely that the incident that caused damage would not ordinarily have happened if proper care and skill had been taken. Examples in the case of railways are:-

- where two trains collide[8]
- where a train leaves the rails[9]; and
- where a train hits the buffers[10].

2.7 It is, of course, open to the defendant railway company to rebut the presumption of negligence by setting out the exact cause of the accident, and requiring the claimant to prove negligence[11].

2.8 If the accident was caused by the deliberate act of a stranger, and this was something which the railway company could not be expected to foresee, then there will be no liability on the railway company. In *Hart v Lancashire and Yorkshire Railway Co.*[12] the claimant was injured when the train in which he was sitting was struck by an engine which had been diverted onto the same track by a points man to avoid a more serious collision. The driver of the engine had collapsed. The court rejected an argument that there should have been two people at the footplate of the engine and found in favour of the defendant railway company. The court also found for the defendant in *Mcdowall v Great Western Railway Co*[13]. The claimant was injured when he was struck by a wagon which had been let loose by trespassing boys. The wagon could have been positioned in a safer location. The court thought it foreseeable that boys would play on the railway, but not that they would set the wagon loose. In this

---

[8] *Ayles v South Eastern Rly Co.* (1868) LR 3 Exch 146
[9] *Dawson v Manchester, Sheffield and Lincolnshire Rly Co.* (1862) 5 LT 682
[10] *Burke v Manchester, Sheffield and Lincolnshire Rly Co.* (1870) 22 LT 442
[11] *Ng Chun Pui v Lee Chuen Tat* [1988] RTR 298
[12] (1869) 21 LT 261
[13] [1903] 2 KB 331

case, there was no evidence called on behalf of the claimant that the wagon should have been put in a safer place.

2.9   The courts' approach to the principle of *res ipsa loquitur* can be seen by looking at a number of cases involving the safety of carriage doors. In *Brooks v LPTB*[14] the court held that it is the duty of a railway company to take reasonable care to see that carriage doors are shut properly before a train leaves the station. An underground train left a station with a door that remained open and the claimant fell out of the carriage. In *Gee v Metropolitan Railway*[15] the claimant leaned against a window and the carriage door opened as a result of which the claimant was injured. The railway company was held liable on the basis that it was under a duty to provide a train in a fit and proper condition with doors properly fastened when starting the journey. The inference was that this was not the case. *Gee* was considered in *Easson v LNE Railway*[16] where it was argued that the burden of proof is on the railway company to explain how a train door came to be open. The court held, however, that it was impossible to say that the doors of an Edinburgh to London express train were under the constant sole control of the railway company for the principal of *res ipsa loquitur* to apply. Passengers were walking up and down the train and getting out at intermediate stations. In this case, there was nothing wrong with the door or the lock and in these circumstances the judge had been entitled to infer that someone had left the door handle open and that the claimant had come out of the lavatory and fallen through the open door onto the line. Finally, in *O'Connor v British Transport Commission*[17] the claimant, an infant aged three years and ten months, was travelling in the guards van of the Holyhead to London train because there were no seats available. The guards van had an

---

[14] [1947] 1 All ER 506
[15] (1873) LR 8 QB 161
[16] [1944] KB 421
[17] [1958] 1 WLR 346

internal handle, designed for the convenience of guards, which opened more easily than the type of handle fitted in passenger compartments. While his mother had left him briefly, the boy opened the door of the guards van, fell out of the train and was fatally injured. The Court of Appeal held that the railway company had been entitled to assume that young children would be accompanied by persons who would take due care in looking after them. It rejected an argument that the railway company had been negligent in having a door handle which could be operated with such ease in a part of the train which was accessible to passengers.

2.10   It should be noted that many of the cases referred to above concern incidents which occurred in the 19th century. This shows that the principles governing the duty owed by railway companies to passengers is longstanding. On the other hand, it is submitted that the cases should now be read with care. For example, in *Hart*, the court expressed the view that the travelling public would be unhappy were the court to decide that the railway company should always have employed two drivers because this would have increased the cost of travel. This perhaps illustrates an approach that might not be followed by modern day courts. Furthermore, the use of carriages with locking sliding doors by railway companies makes the decisions in cases such as *Easson* and *O'Connor* to some extent redundant.

2.11   A modern example of the courts' approach to the duty owed by railway companies to passengers can be seen in *Silverlink Trains Limited v Collins-Williamson*[18]. The claimant, who had been drinking, descended from a train at Gunnersbury Station. He engaged in "*horseplay*", banging on the side of the train, and unfortunately fell between the train and edge of the platform where he was severely injured. It was conceded on behalf of the train company that if the guard did see, or should have seen, the claimant's behaviour while the train

---

[18]   [2009] EWCA Civ 850

was stationary he should not have given the signal for the train to start. The judge considered that the evidence supported the view that the claimant had walked alongside the train for a short period before falling onto the track and that the evidence of timing was such that the claimant's behaviour had started while the train was still stationary and at a time when the guard could have held the train at the station. The Court of Appeal was not prepared to interfere with the judge's finding, although at the same time, it also refused to interfere with the judges finding of 50% contributory negligence.

Safety - Railways and Other Guided Transport Systems (Safety Regulations) 2006[19]

2.12   The Regulations arise out of the directive of the European Parliament and Council 2004/49 on Safety on the Railways in the European Community. It is important to note that the Regulations are made under Section 15 of the Health and Safety at Work Act 1974. Accordingly, a breach of the Regulations does give rise to a cause of action for damages in the civil courts under Section 47(2) of the Health and Safety at Work Act 1974.

2.13   A train operator must have a safety certificate which, under Regulation 7 is issued by the Office of Rail Regulation. The application for a certificate must show the type and extent of the operation and particulars of how the train operator will meet the requirements for the Safety Management System set out in Regulations 5(1) - (4). In essence, the train operator must show that he has a system in place for running a safe railway.

2.14   Under Regulation 5(1), a Safety Management System must ensure that the railway company can achieve the relevant Common Safety Targets, namely the safety levels laid down

---

[19]   SI 2006/599

in the Regulations, and must, in particular, ensure the control of risk to the safety of persons. Under Regulation 5(1)(d)(iii) a Safety Management System must ensure the control of all categories of risk relating to infrastructure of vehicles used on the railway system. The Safety Management System must also meet the elements set out in Schedule 1 to the Regulations which deal with Management and Control of the System. For example, (b) of Schedule 1 says that the Safety Management System shall:

Show how control of the Safety Management System by the management on different levels is secured.

Safety Critical Work

2.15   Regulations 23-26 deal with "*safety critical work*" which concerns the carrying out of safety critical tasks by any person in the course of their work, or in relation to a transport system. Among other things, safety critical tasks include:

- driving a train;
- signalling, and signalling operations;
- installation of components;
- maintenance of the system; and
- ensuring the safety of any persons working on or near to the track.

It is a particular requirement of Regulation 25 that a railway operator must ensure, so far as is reasonably practicable that no worker under his management, supervision or control, carries out safety critical work in circumstances where he is so fatigued, or likely to become so fatigued, that his health or safety, or the health or safety of other persons on the transport system could be significantly affected.

2.16   Most of the Regulations came into force on 10 April 2006 and the remainder on 1 October 2006. Thus a railway company, in order to operate a railway system must establish and maintain a safety management system which meets the requirements of the Regulations and must hold a current safety certificate in relation to the operation in question.

2.17   The Court of Appeal considered the previous regulatory system in *Silverlink Trains Limited v Collins-Williamson*[20]. It was alleged that the Railway Company's method of operation was unsafe and this entailed the court considering the company's "Railway Safety Case" under the Railways (Safety Case) Regulations 2000[21] which were then current at the time of the accident when the claimant fell between the train and the platform. The train comprised class 313 units, the passenger doors being power operated sliding doors which closed at the same time as the guard's door. It was alleged that the railway company should have operated trains with a guard's door which remained open until the train started moving, or with a window through which the guard could look until the train started moving. The company's Railway Safety Case contained a risk assessment which analysed the statistics of passengers falling from platforms which, it was submitted, showed that such incidents were comparatively unusual. The company also pointed to a potential risk of assault on guards if an opening window was provided, although it was submitted on behalf of the claimant that other types of train did provide opening windows for the guard's compartment. The Court of Appeal considered that the absence of evidence of previous accidents in the final 10-20 seconds before a train's departure from a station was an important factor and this, together with the admittedly small risk of injury to guards, meant that the use of Class 313 trains without an opening guard's window did not fall below the standard of care to be expected of a

---

[20]   [2009] EWCA Civ 850
[21]   OSI 2000/2688

railway company. The claim that the railway company's method of operation was negligent therefore failed, although the claimant succeeded on other grounds (see para 2.11).

Level Crossings

2.18   A particular problem for railway companies in the context of safety is that of level crossings. The statutory position governing the creation and operation of level crossings over public highways is now set out in the Level Crossings Act 1983, although, to a certain extent, such level crossings are still covered by earlier statutes as follows:

- Railway Clauses Consolidation Act 1845, which lays down that a railway company should maintain good and sufficient gates across the road on both sides of the railway.
- Railway Clauses Act 1863

For crossings on highways which are not public highways, the relevant statues are:

- Highway (Railway Crossings) Act 1839;
- Railway Regulation Act 1842; and
- Transport Act 1968.

In practice, applications for new protective measures for all public crossings are now made under the Level Crossings Act 1983.

2.19   The common law duty of care was described in *Smith v LMS Railway Co*[22]. There is a duty at every level crossing where there is reason to expect members of the public to be, to take all reasonable precautions to reduce the danger to the public to a minimum. For example, if a level crossing is situated in

---

[22] [1948] SC 136

15

a potentially dangerous place such as a bend in the railway or where a building obscures sight of the rails, the railway company should take steps to make the level crossing safe.

2.20   At common law, a motorist must take care when using a level crossing. Furthermore, the Court of Appeal has said that the duty of a train driver to a person on or approaching a railway line must be distinguished from that of a motorist on a public road. The train driver is on private property and is required to look out for signals and drive to a timetable. The position was set out by Denning LJ in *Lloyds Bank v British Transport Commission*[23] when he said:

> *...you cannot treat a train going along a railway as you can a motor car going along a road. The driver and fireman on an engine must keep a good lookout ahead of them. They must, of course, keep a good lookout for signals and for the track ahead; but they cannot be expected to keep the same lookout for the side road coming up to the railway. They might quite reasonably assume that people who approach a crossing will look out for the trains. Even if the driver sees the headlights of a car, he will assume reasonably that the car would halt and stop for the train to go through. After all, a train cannot be brought to a standstill in much less than half a mile; whereas a car can be brought to a standstill in a few feet.*

2.21   The duty of a railway operator in connection with the provision of a new level crossing was considered by the Court of Session in Scotland in *Rogerson v Network Rail Infrastructure Limited*[24]. In May 2001 there was a serious accident on a level crossing on a private road linking the A9 trunk road to some houses near Pitlochry in Perthshire. The private road crossed the main railway line between Perth and Inverness by a user-worked crossing, which, four years

---

[23] [1956] 3 All ER 291
[24] [2007] CSIH Number 87

earlier, had replaced a crossing that had been operated by an attendant. Railtrack designed the user-worked crossing, carried out safety assessments, and consulted with H.M. Railway Inspectorate. Railtrack produced a draft order in accordance with the Level Crossings Act 1983 and consulted with the local authority, which advertised its proposals. As a result of public representations, a change was made to the design of the crossing to allow operation of the push button controls through the car driver's window. The initial proposal would have involved the driver getting out of his car to use a key to access the controls. Railtrack also carried out a Hazard Operability Study and some concern was expressed about the visibility of the crossing's operating instructions from the driver's seat, but the risk of an accident was considered remote. The problem highlighted by the case was that the crossing's barrier could be raised by the control button even though an approaching train was indicated by a red light and a sounding claxon. It had been suggested that an electronic lock be provided to prevent this happening, but the suggestion was rejected by both Railtrack and H.M. Railways Inspectorate. The driver drove across the track while the red light was shining and claxon sounding, and her passenger was killed. The driver accepted that she had been at fault, but sought contribution from Railtrack.

2.22   The level crossing had been constructed in accordance with the specification included in the Level Crossing Order which had been approved by the Secretary of State under the Level Crossings Act 1983. Railtrack argued that as the Order had been approved by the Secretary of State, they had to comply with it and they relied on an argument that a common law duty of care cannot be imposed on a statutory duty if it is inconsistent with or fetters the statutory duty[25]. The court considered that this was too simplistic an approach. One had to start with the common law duty set out in *Smith*. The court continued:

---

[25] See *X (Minors) v Bedfordshire County Council* [1995] 2 AC 633

No doubt the court cannot impose a duty that flies in the face of a statutory requirement, but among the particular circumstances to which regard requires to be had is the question how the statutory requirement came into existence. Railtrack were no doubt under a statutory duty to comply with the Order, but that is to put the matter too simply. The Order was made at the request of Railtrack, in accordance with the statutory procedure, as operators of the crossing, and they were closely involved at every stage prior to its making. It cannot be suggested that at these stages, they were not subject to the above duty of care.

The judge had criticised Railtrack's failure to place a set of instructions beside the control buttons. The Court of Session considered that this was breach of Railtrack's common law duty of care which could not be avoided by arguing that the making, by the Secretary of State, of the Order relieved them of all liability for negligence in devising the layout of the crossing;

Railtrack's responsibility did not cease with the making of the Order. Their duty of care was continuous and if in the light of experience of its operation any change in the layout of the crossing seemed appropriate, it was Railtrack's responsibility, in discharge of that duty, to request a variation of the Order.

Since the user-worked crossing had come into operation, there had been three "near misses" and the judge had criticised Railtrack for failing to carry out a risk assessment following the third incident. In fact, in the circumstances of the case, Railtrack succeed in defeating the claim for contribution because of its argument on causation, due, at least in part, to concessions which had been made by the driver of the car when she accepted that she had been at fault.

2.23   When an accident occurs at a level crossing as a result of negligence on the part of the motorist, or indeed because the motorist had committed suicide, the railway company, and any passengers injured, may pursue a claim against the motorist's insurers. It is submitted that the motorist's insurance should cover the claim, even in the event of suicide. Section 145 of the Road Traffic Act 1988 provides that insurance must cover:

> *... any liability which may be incurred by him or them in respect of the death of or bodily injury to any person or damage to property caused by, or arising out of, the use of the vehicle on a road in Great Britain.*

Passengers and Visitors at Stations

2.24   The duty owed by a railway company to passengers and visitors at stations is governed by the Occupier's Liability Act 1957. The duty of care under the Act is set out in Section 2, which reads:

> *(1)*   *An occupier of premises owes the same duty, the "common law duty of care", to all his visitors, except insofar as he is free to and does extend, restrict, modify or exclude his duty to any visitor or visitors by agreement or otherwise.*

> *(2)*   *The common law duty of care is a duty to take such care as in all the circumstances of the case is reasonable to see that the visitor will be reasonably safe in using the premises for the purpose for which he is invited or permitted by the occupier to be there.*

2.25   In determining the extent of the common duty of care, a court is entitled to consider, under Section 2(4) of the Occupiers Liability Act 1957 all of the circumstances of the case, to include:

(i) How obvious the danger was;

(ii) Warnings that had been given;

(iii) The adequacy of lighting and the vicinity of the danger;

(iv) The age of the visitor; and

(v) The difficulty and expense of removing the danger.

It is important to note, in particular Section 2(4)(iv), under which the court is invited to accept that a different duty of care is owed in the case of children.

2.26 The freedom to restrict the liability, under Section 2(1) is now limited by the Unfair Contract Terms Act 1977, under which a railway company is not permitted to exclude or restrict liability for death or personal injury resulting from its negligence.

Slipping Accidents at Stations

2.27 A detailed analysis of the circumstances in which occupiers have been held liable under the Occupier's Liability Act is outside the scope of this book. Some guidance can, however, be given. In *Ward v Tesco Stores Ltd*[26], the claimant, who was shopping in the defendant's supermarket slipped on some yoghurt on the floor. The defendant's evidence was that such spillages occurred about 10 times a week and that if a member of staff saw such a spillage they were instructed to stay where they were and arrange for someone to clean the floor. The Court of Appeal held that the defendant had a duty to keep the floors clean and free from spillages. The claimant's accident was not one in the ordinary course of events that would have occurred had the floor been kept clean, or if spillages had been dealt with as they occurred. In the such circumstances, the evidential burden shifted onto the defendant to provide some explanation and to show that the accident had not occurred because of any want of care on

---

[26] [1976] 1 All ER 219

its part. The Court of Appeal held that it was probable that, by the time of the accident, the yoghurt had been on the floor long enough for it to have been cleared up, had there been an adequate inspection and cleaning system in operation. The judge was therefore entitled to infer negligence.

2.28   *Ward* was followed in *Piccolo v Larkstock Limited and Others*[27]. The claimant slipped on a petal outside a flower shop on Marylebone Station. The judge held that the petal should not have been there in the ordinary way, had the floor been kept clean. The burden of proof was therefore on the owner of the flower shop to show that there had been no fault on his part. As the defendant's system was "reactive", where staff cleaned up when notified of a spillage rather than being "pro-active" and cleaning the floor regularly, the judge held in favour of the claimant. He was clearly influenced by the fact that the railway company (which escaped liability) had a systematic cleaning process in operation and had warned the defendant about spillages on several occasions.

2.29   The common duty of care under the Occupier's Liability Act 1957 will extend to taking reasonable steps to clear snow and ice from station platforms. In *Pigford v City of Sunderland*[28], the Court of Appeal contrasted the position where a claimant slipped on a wet pavement with that where the accident was caused by ice. The claimant slipped on a walkway in the defendant's housing estate. There had been previous complaints that the brick block-work surface of the walkway became slippery when wet. The Court of Appeal held the defendants liable because they had done nothing to make the surface of the walkway safer. On the other hand, the court pointed out that if the claimant had, in fact, slipped on ice, there would have been no liability because the defendants could not then be criticised for having failed to grit the walkway by the time of the accident.

---

[27] [Unreported] 7 July 2007
[28] [2003] EWCA Civ 823

2.30   It is submitted that in the case of station platforms, the courts are more likely to follow cases such as *Murphy v City of Bradford Metropolitan Council*[29]. The claimant slipped on a walkway leading from a school car park to the school entrance. The caretaker had put salt on the walkway twice in the two hours before the accident occurred. While the general system of clearing ice employed by the caretaker was considered by the court to be excellent, the location of the accident, on a slope, was important. Stocker LJ said:

The downslope was a very likely place, situated as it was on a smooth surface, for an accident of this type to occur, and therefore it was a candidate for special treatment.

The Court of Appeal found in favour of the claimant on the basis that there had been a failure by the defendants to comply with an otherwise excellent system.

2.31   An example in the case of railways is *Tomlinson v Railway Executive*[30] where there had been heavy snow and a station porter had started to clear snow from the platform, but, in accordance with instructions, he stopped clearing the snow in order to light the station lamps. The claimant, alighting from a train, slipped on the snow and suffered injury. The incident occurred a short time after the snow had fallen and the Court of Appeal held that the railway company was not liable for the accident. Somervell LJ said:

It seems to me it would be an impossible burden on people in the position of the defendants qua snowstorms to say that the snow must be sanded or salted as soon as it falls.

The Court of Appeal considered that reasonable steps to clear the snow were what was required.

---

[29] (Unreported) 29 January 1991
[30] [1953] 1 All ER 1

2.32   It is important to recognise that the duty on railway
        companies extends to arrangements for passengers alighting
        from trains. Railway companies must therefore provide a
        safe means of entering and alighting from trains. In *Foy v
        L.B. and S.C Railway*[31] passengers were asked to alight from
        a train beyond the end of the platform because the train was
        too long for the platform. The railway company was held
        liable as both the place and means of descent from the train
        provided for passengers were not reasonably convenient. A
        train overshooting or not reaching the platform is not
        evidence of negligence. If the passenger chooses to alight
        from the train and is injured then there is no claim.[32] On the
        other hand where a passenger is invited to alight, then there
        will be liability. In *Struthers v British Railway Board*[33] the
        train stopped short of the platform. The station sign had been
        placed where the claimant could see it and this prompted him
        to alight from the train opposite the station sign. The railway
        company was held liable with a finding of one third
        contributory negligence.

Trespassers

2.33   There is a statutory obligation on a railway company to make
        and maintain sufficient fences for separating railway land
        from the adjoining land and for protecting the adjoining land
        from trespass or preventing the cattle of owners and
        occupiers of land from straying by reason of the railway[34].

        The duty is owed only to the owners or occupiers of
        adjoining land. In *Greenhalgh v BRB*[35], an accommodation
        bridge had been built over a cutting where land had been
        severed to make way for a railway. There was a public right
        of way over the accommodation bridge. The local authority

---

[31] (1865) 18 CB (NS) 225
[32] *Siner v GW Rly* (1869) LR 4 PX
[33] (1969) 113S.J268
[34] Section 68 Railway Clauses Consolidation Act 1845
[35] [1969] 2 All ER 114

had built housing on both sides of the railway and had constructed approach roads to each end of the accommodation bridge but it had not repaired the bridge. The claimant suffered an accident while walking over the accommodation bridge. Although she lived in one of the adjacent housing estates, the Court of Appeal held that the claimant did not live close enough to be considered as living on "adjoining land" and accordingly the Railway Clauses Consolidation Act 1845 did not apply. As far as the Railway Company was concerned, the Court of Appeal held that their duty was:

...not to be increased simply because the public choose to use it (the bridge) as a public way and acquire in time a public right to do so.

The Occupiers' Liability Act 1957 did not apply to a right of way following the decision in *Gautret v Egerton* [1867] LR2 CP 371.

2.34   In *Proffitt v British Railways Board*[36], the Court of Appeal was invited to decide that a railway company had a common law duty to fence out trespassers. The claimant's back garden was adjacent to the London to Plymouth railway line. The claimant alleged that although the railway company had erected a fence, this was inadequate to stop her children and their friends crawling through the fence and on to the railway. The Court of Appeal held that there is no common law duty upon a railway company to erect a "teenage-proof fence" so that children cannot climb over the fence on to the railway.

2.35   The question of the duty owed to trespassers developed in connection with the railways. The original, and strict, position was set out in *Robert Addie & Sons (Collieries)*

---

[36] (Unreported) 28 January 1985

Limited v Dumbreck[37]. In that case the House of Lords laid down a general rule that an occupier was under no duty to potential trespassers, whether adults or children, to do anything to protect them from danger on his land, however likely it may be that they will come and run into danger and however lethal the danger may be.

2.36   The law relating to trespassers was considered again in *Videan v British Transport Commission*[38]. A stationmaster's child strayed on to the railway and was run over by a train. The Court of Appeal held that the claimant, a child, was a trespasser and that the railway company was not liable. Following the decision in *Addie*, no duty at all arose until the trespassers were known to be on the land or where the occupier should have known that the trespassers were on his land.

2.37   The position of trespassers was considered further by the House of Lords in *British Railways Board v Herrington*[39]. The railway company owned an electrified line which was fenced off from a meadow where children lawfully played. In 1965 the fence had been in a dilapidated condition for several months and this was known to the railway company. It had also been reported that children had been seen playing on the railway nearby. The claimant, aged six, trespassed over the broken fence from the meadow where he had been playing, and was injured on the live rail. The House of Lords considered that the earlier decision in *Addie* should be overruled because it had been rendered obsolete by changes in physical and social conditions. There was less space for children to play and a greater temptation for them to trespass. With the progress of technology there were more and greater dangers and considerably more need for occupiers to take reasonable steps to deter persons,

---

[37] [1929] AC 358
[38] [1963] 2 QB 650
[39] [1972] 2 WLR 537

especially children, from trespassing in dangerous places. In the circumstances the House of Lords decided that the railway company did owe a duty to the claimant child to take such steps as common sense or common humanity would dictate to exclude or warn, or otherwise, within reasonable and practical limits, to reduce or avert danger.

Trespassers - Occupiers' Liability Act 1984

2.38   The duty of an occupier to persons other than his visitors is now covered by the Occupiers' Liability Act 1984. Under Section 1(1) of the Act, a Court must consider whether there was a risk of such a person suffering injury on the premises:

(a) *by reason of any danger due to the state of the premises or to things done or omitted to be done on them.*

The Act then says (Section 1(3)) that an occupier owes a duty to someone who is not his visitor in respect of any such risk if:

(a) *he is aware of the danger or has reasonable grounds to believe that it exists;*
(b) *he knows or has reasonable grounds to believe that the other is in the vicinity of the danger concerned or that he may come into the vicinity of the danger ...; and*
(c) *the risk is one against which, in all the circumstances of the case, he may reasonably be expected to offer the other some protection.*

2.39   The Occupiers' Liability Act 1984 was considered by the Court of Appeal in *Keown v Coventry Healthcare NHS Trust*[40]. The defendant owned premises which it knew attracted children who used to play on two fire escapes. The claimant, an 11-year-old boy, climbed the underside of the fire escape, fell and was severely injured. The Court of

---

[40] [2006] EWCA Civ 39

Appeal considered that under the Act the claimant could not have succeeded if he were an adult. Did it make a difference that the claimant was a child? There was evidence that the claimant appreciated that what he was doing was dangerous and that he should not have been climbing the exterior of the fire escape. In the circumstances, the Court of Appeal considered that the danger did not arise out of the state of the premises, which were as one would expect them to be. Rather, the danger arose out of what the claimant chose to do.

2.40   The Court of Appeal went on to say that it would have been prepared to hold that the defendant had knowledge of the foresight of the danger and of the presence of the trespasser. It considered, however, that this was not a case where the defendant might reasonably be expected to have offered some protection. If it had had to offer some protection against falling from the fire escape, the NHS Trust would have had to consider protection against falling from drainpipes, balconies and roofs. This would be a drain on limited NHS resources. Although it is submitted that the Court of Appeal would have decided in the same way should a similar claim be brought against a railway company, nevertheless it is arguable that when dealing with the last point, the Court of Appeal might have decided differently and said that a railway company could be expected to offer protection against the risk of injury.

Contribution

2.41   It is open to a railway company to seek a contribution or indemnity from another party who has caused damage or injury either to passengers or indeed to a train itself. The case of *Great North Eastern Railway Limited v Hart*[41] concerned a serious accident which occurred when the defendant fell asleep while driving along the M62 motorway

---

[41] (Unreported) 30 October 2003

and his vehicle ended up on the main railway between Newcastle and London, causing a serious rail disaster. Claims were brought by the railway company and passengers against the defendant and indeed this was, in fact, a claim by the defendant driver against the Secretary of State for Transport, Local Government and the Regions, claiming a contribution towards damages claimed by the victims of the accident and the claimant railway company. It was alleged that a longer safety barrier should have been erected at the railway bridge and that this would have prevented the accident. Moreland J decided that there had been no negligence on the part of the Department when the safety fencing was originally constructed because it had complied with the relevant minimum standards at the time of construction. The judge accepted evidence that the site would not have been identified as representing a risk which was out of the ordinary. The decision in *Stovin v Wise*[42] would not have been an answer to the claim relating to the original construction of the safety barrier, but was an answer to the claim alleging that the Department did have the power to alter the length of the safety fencing but had failed to take any action.

2.42   Another example is to be found in *Health & Safety Executive v Thames Trains Limited*[43]. The case was concerned with the disastrous accident at Ladbroke Grove outside Paddington Station, when a First Great Western train collided with a train operated by Thames Trains, whose driver had missed a red signal. It should be noted that there was no issue between the victims of the accident, the passengers, and either Thames Trains or Railtrack. Thames Trains had agreed to try to settle the personal injury claims. As Waller LJ said:

So far as the victims are concerned, there was obviously a strong case on liability against Thames Trains and further, a

---

[42] [1996] AC 923
[43] [2003] EWCA Civ 720

*strong case against Railtrack, relating to inadequacies in the
signalling system.*

2.43   The Court of Appeal was dealing with a claim by Thames
Trains, seeking contribution and/or indemnity from the
Health & Safety Executive who had a regulatory role in
approving alterations to tracks and signalling. The Court of
Appeal agreed with the judge that the Health & Safety
Executive did not owe a statutory duty which gave rise to a
private right to claim damages. It was arguable, however,
that the Health & Safety Executive owed a common law duty
of care arising out of the statutory power or duty to inspect.
The Court relied on the House of Lords' decision in *Stovin*.
In that case the House of Lords had, by a majority, decided
in favour of the defendant Highway Authority but had
indicated that a duty of care could arise out of the existence
of a statutory power if it would have been irrational not to
have exercised the power, and where there were exceptional
grounds for holding that the policy of the statute required
compensation to be paid to persons who suffered loss
because the power was not exercised.

2.44   Although the Court of Appeal was not convinced that the
case against the Health & Safety Executive was confined to
"omissions" alone (and this may be important), nevertheless
the Court of Appeal took the view that passengers would rely
on the Health & Safety Executive performing its duty and
that accordingly, there were exceptional grounds for holding
that the policy of the statute required compensation to be
paid. Furthermore the Court of Appeal considered that the
non-performance of the statutory power could be regarded as
being "irrational".

2.45   It is, however, significant to note that in the later case of
Gorringe v Calderdale Metropolitan Borough Council[44], the

---

[44] [2004] UKHL 15, [2004] 1 WLR 1057

House of Lords took the view that its earlier decision in *Stovin* had been misunderstood. Lord Hoffman said:

Speaking for myself, I find it difficult to imagine a case in which a common law duty can be founded simply upon the failure (however irrational) to provide some benefit which a public authority has power (or a public law duty) to provide ... My Lords, in this case, the council is not alleged to have done anything to give rise to a duty of care. The complaint is that it did nothing. Section 39 of the Road Traffic Act 1988 gives the sole ground on which it is alleged to have had a common law duty to act. In my opinion the statute could not have created such a duty.

2.46   In the circumstances it is possible that if the Court of Appeal had heard the case against the Health & Safety Executive following the decision in *Gorringe*, it might have come to a different conclusion. On the other hand, the decision might perhaps stand on the basis that, given the facts of the case, the claim against the Health & Safety Executive raised allegations of positive acts and not on omissions alone.

Nuisance

2.47   There are two forms of nuisance: private and public nuisance. They have been described as follows:

Nuisance is an act or omission which is an interference, disturbance or annoyance to a person in the exercise or enjoyment of:

(i)   *the right belonging to him as a member of the public, when it is a public nuisance, or*

(ii)   *his ownership or occupation of land or some easement, profit, or other right used or enjoyed in connection with land, when it is a private nuisance*[45].

---

[45] Clerk & Lindsell on Torts (Sweet & Maxwell, 19th Edition, 2006), para 20-1

2.48   Because railway companies operate under statutory authority, under Section 122 of the Railways Act 1993, there is a defence to actions in nuisance arising out of the user of rolling stock or any track used by a railway company.

2.49   It is relevant to consider the law of nuisance in relation to railways by reference to the potential damage caused by trees.

2.50   First, under Section 24 of the Regulation of Railways Act 1868, a railway company may obtain an order from a Magistrates' Court that a landowner must remove any tree standing near a railway if it is in danger of falling on to the railway so as to obstruct the traffic.

2.51   The position in relation to trees falling on a highway, and it is submitted that, by analogy, this must also relate to trees falling on to railways, was considered in the case of *Caminer & Another v Northern & London Investment Trust Limited*[46]. A large tree growing in the defendant's property fell on to the plaintiff's car, damaging it and injuring the plaintiff. The tree, which was about 130 years old, carried a considerable crown, although not abnormal for a tree of that age, and had never been lopped, topped or pollarded. Evidence was given that the tree should have been inspected every five or seven years and that if the tree had been topped, it was unlikely that it would have fallen when it did, but that the tree did not appear to be dangerous before the accident. The House of Lords decided that in the absence of evidence that the defendant had failed in his duty to take reasonable care, it was not liable. An external examination of the tree could not have revealed its diseased condition, and their Lordships did not consider that there was any duty on the landowner to bore into the trunk of the tree to ascertain its condition in the absence of any other signs of disease. The claims, whether framed in negligence or nuisance, failed because the

---

[46] [1950] 2 All ER 486

necessary elements of foreseeability and knowledge were absent.

2.52   On the other hand, in a similar case, *Chapman v London Borough of Barking & Dagenham*[47], the Court of Appeal upheld the judge's decision against the highway authority. During a period of very high winds in January 1990, a branch from a tree in the highway fell on to the plaintiff's van, causing him serious injury. A duty to inspect the tree seems to have been accepted by the defendant and this would seem to follow from the decision in *Caminer* above. The judge, therefore, had to decide whether there was a breach of duty, and this question turned on whether a reasonable system of inspection would have revealed that the tree was diseased before the accident occurred. The judge accepted evidence that after the tree had been felled following the accident, the stump had shown signs of decay. The presence of active bacteria in the decay showed that there must have been an open wound on the tree. The judge also held that there would have been decay at the fork in the tree, where the branches grew out of the trunk. It was accepted that this decay could only have been seen by a "climbing inspection" of the tree.

2.53   The judge held that there was a clear duty on the defendant to conduct a "systematic expert inspection" of the trees on or close to the highway. In fact, the defendant had not carried out any formal inspection, certainly following the October 1987 gale (which the tree had survived). The judge was satisfied that an inspection from ground level should have been carried out before 1990 when the accident occurred. Liability in the case then depended upon whether such an inspection would have revealed anything which would have shown that a "climbing inspection" of the tree was necessary. The judge decided in favour of the plaintiff because the tree was in a busy area, which should have been high on any tree

---

[47] [1998] CLY 4053

inspection programme. Various pruning wounds, which the judge held to be a potentially hazardous source of infection, were visible from ground level and were located at the fork in the tree, where water would be particularly likely to collect. Although the Court of Appeal was urged to overturn the decision on the basis that the judge had misinterpreted the evidence, it refused to interfere with the decision.

2.54   The approach to be adopted by a landowner in respect of his trees has been considered more recently in *Poll v Viscount Asquith of Morley*[48]. A motorcyclist collided with a branch which had fallen down on to a road from a tree on the defendant's land. Although the tree had been inspected, the Court held that the landowner should have employed a more experienced tree expert who would have appreciated that, although the defect which caused the branch to fall was difficult to observe, nevertheless the fact that the tree was multi-stemmed merited a more detailed inspection by a properly qualified tree expert.

2.55   An example of a public nuisance is to be found in *Wandsworth London Borough Council v Railtrack Plc*[49]. Pigeons were roosting under the defendant's railway bridge, fouling the pavement below with their droppings, and causing considerable inconvenience to pedestrians. Railtrack argued that because the pigeons proliferated due to the local community providing food, the local authority should exercise its power under Section 74 of the Public Health Act 1961 to abate the nuisance. The Court of Appeal held, however, that the liability of Railtrack as landowner did not depend on whether the nuisance was created by its own or a third party's activities or by natural causes. Railtrack were liable because they were aware of the existence of the nuisance, had the means and opportunity to abate it and had failed to do so. Kennedy LJ said:

---

[48] (Unreported) 11 May 2006
[49] [2001] EWCA Civ 1236, [2003] QB 756

... it is clear beyond argument that interference with the right of the public to enjoy the highway in reasonable comfort and convenience can amount to a public nuisance ... where there is a public nuisance on the defendant's land, it does not matter whether it was created by the defendant or some third party, or by natural causes ... if the defendant is aware of it, has had a reasonable opportunity to abate it, has the means to abate it, and has chosen not to do so, then he is liable, and there is no reason to approach the matter as though it were a claim in negligence or private nuisance.

THREE

EMPLOYER'S LIABILITY

Introduction

3.1   Both at common law and by statute, or statutory regulation, an employer owes a duty of reasonable care to its employees. From the point of view of the protection given to employees, these duties have been significantly enhanced by the intervention of the European Union, principally in terms of Directives implemented in the United Kingdom in the form of a series of regulations passed from 1992 onwards.

3.2   Unlike the common law duty to take reasonable care, many of these statutory duties are absolute. The introduction of these duties has combined with the court's willingness to interpret the law widely (in particular the meaning of the words 'employee' and 'equipment') to create a health and safety environment which has moved a considerable way in favour of protecting the employee and calls for greater vigilance on the part of the employer. Indeed, cases in this chapter, which were decided before the introduction of the Regulations based on the European Directives, should probably be read with care.

The Common Law Duty of Care

3.3   The introductory chapter outlines the fundamental principles of the law of negligence. It is also appropriate to refer to the House of Lords' three-stage approach in the case of *Caparo*

Industries Plc v Dickman.[50] In order for liability to be established, the requirements are as follows:

- foreseeability of damage;
- relationship of proximity between the parties; and
- it is just and reasonable that the law should impose a duty in the circumstances of the case.

3.4   There is no doubt that the relationship between employer and employee is an instance where these three criteria will be met and a duty of care will arise. An employer has a duty to take reasonable care for the safety of its employees. The duty is usually broken down as follows:

(i)   to provide the employee with a safe place of work, including safe access to that place of work;

(ii)   to provide the employee with a proper system of work (including proper training and supervision);

(iii)   to provide the employee with plant, machinery or equipment adequate for the task; and

(iv)   to provide the employee with competent fellow employees.

3.5   Case-law has shown that in many instances these duties overlap; for example, on a training course the duty to provide a safe system of work may involve a duty to provide proper supervision as well as to provide competent colleagues.

3.6   An employer's duty to each employee is non-delegable. Thus liability cannot be avoided simply because an employee is working under the supervision of a third party or whilst visiting premises belonging to a member of the public.

3.7   Provided the requirements for liability are satisfied, an employer will be liable for all recognised forms of injury,

---

[50]   [1990] 2 AC 605

namely physical injury (including work-related upper limb disorders and vibration white finger), industrial disease, occupational deafness and psychiatric damage (including psychiatric damage caused by stress in the workplace) if it meets the other conditions for liability.

3.8   An employee may himself be negligent, or in breach of statutory duty, and the principles relating to contributory negligence and the maxim *'volenti non fit injuria'* have to be considered. It must be noted, however, that the defence of *volenti non fit injuria* has very limited application in employer's liability cases.

3.9   As mentioned in the introduction, the employer's duty of care to the employee is non-delegable. The duty is also personal to each individual employee. A good example of this is the case of *Paris v Stepney Borough Council.*[51] The claimant, employed by the defendant local authority as a garage hand, had only one good eye. During the course of his employment he sustained an injury to that eye and claimed that whilst it may not have been necessary for the majority of garage hands, the defendant had been under a duty to provide the claimant with goggles to protect his remaining good eye. The defendant argued that the risk of an accident occurring was the same for workers with both eyes as it was for the claimant, and that the severity of the injury was irrelevant to the determination of the existence or scope of the duty.

3.10   That proposition was rejected by the House of Lords. Lord Simmons (actually dissenting on the facts) said:

The issue, my Lords, is narrowed down and I will say at once that I do not dissent from the view that an employer owes a particular duty to each of his employees. His liability in tort arises from his failure to take reasonable care in relation to the particular employee and it is clear that, if so, all the

---

[51]   [1951] AC 367

circumstances relevant to that employee must be taken into consideration. I see no valid reason for excluding as irrelevant the gravity of the damage which the employee will suffer if an accident occurs...

3.11   An employer's common law duties are supplemented by duties imposed by legislation, much of which brings into English law the various European Directives on health and safety at work. Breach of most (but not all) of these statutory duties will give rise to a civil liability for damages. The extent of the duties imposed by statute is relevant when assessing the reasonableness of an employer's conduct. The existence of a statutory duty may, therefore, in appropriate circumstances be used as a guide in a claim brought in negligence. For example, if Parliament has provided that a particular activity carries a risk to health and safety against which an employer should guard, it cannot be said that the danger is not reasonably foreseeable by a prudent employer. Furthermore, if an injury is caused by defective equipment provided by the employer for the purposes of its business, the employer will be liable to the employee for that defect even if the fault for it lies elsewhere (Employer's Liability Defective Equipment Act 1969).

The impact of Europe

3.12   A number of Directives with relevance to health and safety have been produced in Europe and largely implemented in the United Kingdom by a number of different regulations, mostly passed to take effect from 1 January 1993. These were the Framework Directive 89/391/EEC and the six consequent Directives:

(i)   The Workplace (the 1st) Directive 9/654/EEC;

(ii)   The Work Equipment (the 2nd) Directive 89/655/EEC;

(iii)   The Personal Protective Equipment (the 3rd) Directive 89/656/EEC;

(iv)   The Manual Handling of Heavy Loads (the 4th) Directive 90/269/EEC;

(v)   The Display Screen Equipment (the 5th) Directive 90/270/EEC; and

(vi)   The Carcinogens (the 6th) Directive 90/394/EEC.

3.13   The current regulations in the United Kingdom, which were derived, principally from the Directives are:

(i)   the Management of Health and Safety at Work Regulations 1999;[52]

(ii)   the Provision and Use of Work Equipment Regulations 1998;[53]

(iii)   the Workplace (Health, Safety and Welfare) Regulations 1992;[54]

(iv)   the Personal Protective Equipment at Work Regulations 1992;[55]

(v)   the Manual Handling Operations Regulations 1992[56];

(vi)   the Health and Safety (Display Screen Equipment) Regulations 1992;[57]

(vii)   the Control of Substances Hazardous to Health Regulations 2002;[58] and

(viii) the Control of Asbestos at Work Regulations 2002.[59]

A number of these Regulations have been supplemented by approved codes of practice.

3.14   In the context of railways it is also important to consider the *Railways and Other Guided Transport Systems (Safety)*

---

[52] SI 1999/3242
[53] SI 1998/2307
[54] SI 1992/3004
[55] SI 1992/2966
[56] SI 1992/2792
[57] SI 1992/2793
[58] SI 2002/2677
[59] SI 2002/2675

Regulations 2006[60]. These reproduce, in part, the Directive of the European Parliament and Council 2004/49 on Safety on the Community's Railways.

3.15   The Regulations set out in paragraphs 3.13 and 3.14 above were made under S.15 of the Health and Safety at Work Act 1974 and breach of the Regulations is actionable by any person thereby caused damage under S.47(2) of the same Act.

3.16   There has been criticism from some lawyers that the regulations set out in paragraph 3.13 above do not fully implement the corresponding European Directives because they often limit the employer's duty by the words 'so far as reasonably practicable' or equivalent, when no such words of limitation appear in the Directives. 'Reasonably practicable' is a phrase which has appeared in domestic health and safety legislation for many decades. Asquith LJ considered its meaning in the case of *Edwards v National Coal Board*[61]. He said:

Reasonably practicable" is a narrower term than "physically possible" and seems to me to imply that a computation must be made by the owner, in which the quantum of risk is placed on one scale and the sacrifice involved in the measures necessary for averting the risk (whether in money, time or trouble) is placed in the other, and that if it be shown that there is a gross disproportion between them - the risk being insignificant in relation to the sacrifice - the defendants discharge the onus on them

Nevertheless, whilst the employer's duty is limited by the words 'reasonably practicable', the burden on an employer to prove that everything reasonably practical has been done is a heavy one.

---

[60]   SI 2006/599
[61]   [1949] 1 KB 704

3.17   If a regulation fails properly to implement a Directive a claimant may have recourse to the Directive itself. To date, claims based on an alleged failure to implement a European Directive have not succeeded:

    (i)   In *Sussex Ambulance NHS Trust v King,*[62] the Court of Appeal held that there was no discrepancy between the relevant parts of the Manual Handling Operations Regulations 1992 and the Directive which they sought to implement.

    (ii)   In *Stark v Post Office,*[63] the Court of Appeal accepted that the European Directive, under which the Provision and Use of Work Equipment Regulations 1992 were made, did not require the English Regulations to impose an absolute obligation in respect of the maintenance of work equipment, but held that in that respect Parliament had gone beyond the requirements of the Directive (as it was indeed entitled to do).

Specific duties owed

Place of work

3.18   At common law, the place of work encompasses the whole range of workplaces, including both those workplaces of which the employer is the occupier and those of which it is not. With regards to the latter, the employer may need to carry out an inspection of the site of the work so as to satisfy itself that it is safe, and provide the employee with any necessary warnings and ensure that any dangers are ameliorated by any necessary protective clothing or by any equipment.

---

[62]   [2002] EWCA CIV 953
[63]   [2000] ICR 1013

3.19   The requirement for a safe place of work extends to the means of access to the place of work. This is illustrated by those cases where the employee trips or slips on a dangerous substance in the hallway or on steps leading to the place of work.

3.20   The common law duty is not absolute. It is a duty to take reasonable care to ensure that the place of work is safe. The common law duty has, however, been greatly strengthened by the imposition of statutory duties relating to the workplace, where the duties are frequently absolute. Indeed, earlier cases which were decided in common law negligence, should be read with caution. Early examples of statutory duties were the duties imposed by the Factories Act 1961 and, more obviously, the Offices, Shops and Railway Premises Act 1963. Both of these statutes have been largely repealed by (amongst others) the various Regulations passed in 1992 to implement the European Directives.

The Workplace (Health, Safety and Welfare) Regulations 1992

3.21   With some exclusions, the Workplace (Health, Safety and Welfare) Regulations 1992 apply to every workplace and every employer. They lay down obligations in relation to maintenance of the workplace and its equipment, ventilation, temperature, lighting, cleanliness and waste materials, workstations, heating, floors and traffic routes. For the most part, these duties are absolute (the requirement to maintain the workplace and its equipment in an efficient state, efficient working order and in good repair, for example, and to provide ventilation and lighting), although some involve limited elements of reasonable practicality (in particular, the duty to take effective measures to prevent persons falling a distance likely to cause personal injury or being struck by a falling object).

3.22 The Workplace (Health, Safety and Welfare) Regulations 1992 were considered by the Court of Appeal in *Furness v Midland Bank plc.*[64] The claimant slipped on a very small amount of water on the stairs. There was no known previous history of water being there and no one was able to say how it got there on that particular occasion. Under reg 12(3) the employer was obliged, so far as reasonably practicable, to keep the floor free from substances 'which might cause a person to slip'. The trial judge held that the only way to ensure that the stairs remained free from substances would be to post someone on guard and that such an action would be wholly disproportionate to the very small risk and therefore not within the bounds of reasonable practicability. The Court of Appeal agreed with the trial judge, adding that an instruction to staff to keep an eye out for spillages would have been futile, particularly given the lack of any history of such spillages.

3.23 The same Regulations were considered again in *Lewis v Avidan Ltd.*[65] The claimant, a care assistant in a nursing home, slipped and fell on a patch of water in the hallway of the nursing home. The water had come from a concealed pipe which had burst shortly before the accident. No one had been aware of the burst pipe or the patch of water on the floor. Looking at the Regulations, the term 'workplace' clearly included the floor of the nursing home as the claimant had access to it while at work. On the other hand, 'workplace' did not include the enclosed pipe. There was no negligence proved against the defendant and accordingly the floor was maintained, for the purpose of reg 5, in an efficient state. Even if the pipe amounted to 'equipment' for reg 5, the unexpected flood did not mean that the floor was not in an efficient state, in efficient working order and in good repair for the purpose of reg 5.

---

[64] (Unreported) 10 November 2000, CA
[65] (Unreported) 13 April 2005, CA

3.24   On the other hand, in *Robinson v Midland Bank plc* [66] the claimant fell over a moveable stool used for gaining access to high shelves. She had passed the site of the accident shortly before. She returned carrying files which obstructed her view. The stool had, in the meantime, been moved by another employee. The claimant did not see the stool and fell over. Regulation 12(3) was again in issue. The judge dismissed the claim on the basis that the stool, by its very function, had to be moved from place to place and that the claimant should have kept a lookout. The Court of Appeal, however, allowed the claimant's appeal (and made no reduction for contributory negligence), holding that it was well within the bounds of reasonable practicability for the stool to be kept out of the path of the claimant, or at least for a warning to be given if it had to be left in a position where it was a potential hazard.

3.25   A quite different approach to Regulation 12 was taken by the Court of Appeal in *Ellis v Bristol City Council.* [67] The claimant worked in a home for the elderly and infirm, where she slipped on a pool of urine. There had been a risk assessment and suggested preventive measures had been taken before the accident. The Court of Appeal, instead of considering the "reasonable practicality" test under Regulation 12(3) (see para. 3.22 above) decided the case under the strict liability positions in Regulation 12(1) and (2) which provide that every floor in a workplace <u>shall</u> be of a construction such that the surface is suitable for the purpose for which it is used. Smith LJ considered that Regulations 12(1) and (2) were not limited to a floor which was in a permanent state of slipperiness, but, also applied to a slipperiness which occurred frequently:

> *If a smooth floor is frequently and regularly slippery, because of a substance which lies upon it, albeit only*

---

[66]   (Unreported) 27 October 2000
[67]   [2007] EWCA Civ 685

temporarily, the surface of the floor may properly be said to be unsuitable, lithe slipperiness is such as to give rise to a risk to the health and safety of those employees using it.

Factors in judging the suitability of a floor surface under Regulation 12(1) would, according to Smith LJ, include:

The construction of the floor, including the nature or quality of its surface. They will include the purposes for which the floor was used, and the circumstances of use.

Although Lloyd LJ considered that there was force in the argument that transient problems are governed by Regulation 12(3) and not by Regulation 12(1), nevertheless, he agreed with Smith LJ's approach to Regulation 12(1). The Court of Appeal went on to assess the claimant's contributory negligence at one third.

3.26   The Health and Safety (Display Screen Equipment) Regulations 1992 provide protection to employees who habitually use display screen equipment as part of their normal work. The central duty imposed upon the employer is to perform an analysis of workstations used for the purpose of his undertaking so as to assess the health and safety risks of that use with a view to reducing those risks to the lowest extent reasonably practicable.

3.27   The requirement for a risk assessment is also an important obligation under the Control of Substances Hazardous to Health Regulations, 2002. The central obligation is contained in Regulation 7(1):

Every employer shall ensure that the exposure of his employees to substances hazardous to health is either prevented or, where this is not reasonably practicable, adequately controlled.

In *Dugmore v Swansea NHS Trust,*[68] the Court of Appeal held that both the primary duty of preventing exposure and the secondary duty of adequate control (where prevention is not reasonably practicable) were effectively absolute. Hale LJ said:

'Adequately' is defined in Regulation 7 without any reference to reasonableness or foreseeability of risk; it is a purely practical matter depending upon the nature of the substance and the nature and degree of the exposure and nothing else.

System of work

Common law

3.28   In common law the duty to provide a safe system of work applies to all work situations including training, instructions on the requirements for a particular task, the methods adopted, the provision of sufficient numbers of workers for the task, the availability of assistance and proper planning, supervision and coordination.

3.29   As with the place of work, the employer's common law duty to provide a safe system of work is not absolute. Thus, in *Brodie v Kent County Council*[69], carers working in an old people's home who had suffered from back problems were told to stay away from work until their doctor passed them fit to return. The claimant did not consult her doctor about her return and hurt her back during the course of lifting an elderly resident from the floor. The Court of Appeal held that the system was safe and that there was no duty to secure

---

[68]   [2002] EWCA Civ 1689, [2003] ICR 573. The Court of Appeal was considering earlier versions of the regulations, but with no material difference in the words.
[69]   (Unreported) 14 February 1986 CA

the use of lifting equipment. Each case will of course depend on its own facts.

3.30   The duty to provide a safe system of work is not satisfied by simply requiring the employee to read and adhere to written instructions. In *Barcock v Brighton Corporation,*[70] the claimant was employed at the defendant's electricity substation. There was a written procedure for shutting down the switchboard safely; however, the claimant's supervisors used to ignore this procedure, thus introducing an element of risk. When he took over the job, the claimant continued to follow the unsafe system of work. The claimant suffered an accident. The court held that the defendant could not demonstrate a safe system of work merely by handing the claimant a copy of the written procedure and telling him to comply with it. Furthermore, the written procedure had long been ignored by the claimant's supervisors.

3.31   There is a duty to ensure that the prescribed system is complied with. In *Pape v Cumbria County Council*[71], it was held that a reasonable employer, knowing that sustained exposure to cleaning agents meant a risk of dermatitis or eczema and appreciating that the risk was not so well known to employees, should take steps to ensure that the gloves were supplied with a warning, which should include an explanation of the danger involved and the reasons for the need to wear gloves.

3.32   A different situation arises where the employee knows about a risk to his health, but still wishes to continue doing the same job. *Coxall v Goodyear GB Limited*[72] considered the general principle to be found in *Withers v Perry Chain Co Ltd.*[73] In *Withers*, the claimant suffered from dermatitis. She

[70]   [1949] 1 KB 339
[71]   [1992] ICL 132
[72]   [2002] EWCA Civ 1010, [2003] 1 WLR 536
[73]   [1961] 1 WLR 1313

returned to work even though it was known both to her and her employer that if she continued to work there was a small risk that her condition would be exacerbated. When the condition did indeed deteriorate, the claimant brought an action for damages. The Court of Appeal allowed the employer's appeal on the basis that it would be an unwarranted restriction on individual freedom if an employer were effectively required to dismiss an employee in order to obviate a slight risk of injury. In *Coxall*, the Court of Appeal, while not seeking to overrule the decision in *Withers*, decided in favour of the employee in a case where his continuing to work in a paint store caused him to suffer a severe asthmatic condition. Although the employee knew the risk and had decided that he wanted to continue to work in the paint store, the Court of Appeal found the employer liable. It considered that, where the risk was of serious harm, an employer might not be entitled to allow an employee to continue working. Furthermore the employee's damages were not reduced to take into account contributory negligence.

3.33   The decisions in *Withers* and *Coxall* should no doubt also be considered against the background of the duties on employers provided by the Disability Discrimination Act 1995.

3.34   The duty to warn an employee of a specific risk arising out of his employment depends upon the circumstances and the nature of the job involved. For example, in *Koonjul v Thameslink Healthcare Services*[74] the Court of Appeal considered that telling someone how to make a bed involved so mundane a task that instruction was not necessary. On the other hand, in *O'Neill v DSG Retail*[75] it was considered that the defendant had been negligent in failing to warn about the risk of making an instinctive response while carrying a

---

[74]   [2000] PIQR 123
[75]   [2002] EWCA Civ 1139, [2003] ICR 223

heavy load. The duty, and question of breach, will depend upon the circumstances.

The Manual Handling Operations Regulations 1992

3.35   The Manual Handling Operations Regulations 1992 came into effect on 1 January 1993. They regulate all manual handling operations, meaning 'any transporting or supporting of a load (including the lifting, putting down, pushing, pulling, carrying or moving thereof) by hand or by bodily force'. 'Load' includes any person or any animal. The definition of a manual handling operation is wide — the courts have held that shovelling grit on ice and slipping whilst on ungritted ice amounts to such an operation *(King v RCQ Support Services)*[76], and also that that a teacher grabbing an unruly child is a manual handling operation *(Purves v Buckingham County Council)*[77]. There is, however, a limit as to what is a manual handling operation - repetitive packing of crisp bags was not a manual handling operation *(Gissing v Walkers Smiths Snack Foods Limited)*[78]. Likewise, the pushing and pulling when working with a spanner to loosen and tighten bolts on production machinery did not amount to the transporting or supporting of a load *(King v Carron Phoenix Limited)*[79].

3.36   The employer's duty under the Regulations is contained in reg 4 which states as follows:

(1)   Each employer shall:

(a)   so far as is reasonably practicable avoid the need for his employees to undertake any

---

[76]   [2001] PIQR P 206
[77]   (Unreported) 20 November 1998
[78]   [1999] CLY 3983
[79]   [1999] REP LR 51

(b)   manual handling operations at work which involve a risk of their being injured; or

(b)   where it is not reasonably practicable to avoid the need for his employees to undertake any manual handling operations at work which involve a risk of their being injured:

    (i)   make a suitable and sufficient risk assessment of all such manual handling operations to be undertaken by them, having regard to the factors which are specified in Column 1 of Schedule 1 to these Regulations and considering the questions which are specified in the corresponding entry in Column 2 of that Schedule,

    (ii)   take appropriate steps to reduce the risk of injury to those employees arising out of their undertaking any such manual handling operations to the lowest level reasonably practicable, and

    (iii)   take appropriate steps to provide any of those employees who are undertaking any such manual handling operations with general indications, and where it is not reasonably practical so to do so, to provide precise information on:

        (aa)   The weight of the load, and

        (bb)   The heaviest side of the load whose centre of gravity is not positioned centrally.

(2)   Any assessment, such as is referred to in paragraph
         (1)(b)(i) of this Regulation, shall be reviewed by the
         employer who made it if:

    (a)   there is reason to suspect that it is no longer
                 valid; or
    (b)   there has been a significant change in the
                 manual handling operations to which it
                 relates; and where, as a result of such
                 review, changes to an assessment are
                 required, the relevant employer shall make
                 them.

3.37   The assessment must be carried out with regard to a number
       of factors listed in questions asked in Sch 1 to the
       Regulations. The factors are the tasks, the loads, the working
       environment and the capacity of the individual, together with
       any other factors, and a number of questions should be asked
       in relation to each.

Reasonably practicable

3.38   It is important to note that the first point raised under reg
       4(1)(a) is that an employer should avoid the need for its
       employees to carry out manual handling unless it is not
       reasonably practicable to avoid such manual handling.

3.39   The courts have considered when it will, and will not, be
       reasonably practicable to avoid the need for an employee to
       engage in manual handling which involves a risk of injury.
       In *Hawkes v London Borough of Southwark*[80] the claimant
       was injured while carrying a door upstairs. It would, in
       theory, have been possible for the claimant to have used
       some mechanical lifting device, but the reality was that such
       a device was not reasonably practicable. The Court of
       Appeal, however, held that it would have been reasonably

---

[80]   (Unreported) 20 February 1998.

practicable to engage a second worker to assist the claimant in carrying the door. Reasonable practicability involves a balancing exercise between the likelihood of injury occurring together with the likely severity of such injury that might occur balanced against the cost in time, effort and money in trying to eliminate the risk of injury altogether.

3.40   The case of *Sussex Ambulance NHS Trust v King*[81] concerned the Manual Handling Operations Regulations 1992 and the Provision and Use of Work Equipment Regulations 1992. The claimant, an ambulance man, was assisting a colleague in taking a heavy patient from a restricted upstairs' space. They carried the patient downstairs and the claimant injured his back. It was alleged that the answer should have been to call on the fire brigade to take the patient out of the bedroom through a window. The Court of Appeal rejected the claim that there had been a breach of the regulations, as there was nothing to suggest there had been any breach. There was a balance to be drawn, judged by the risk involved. There was no evidence before the court that the ambulance service could have done anything to limit the risk to its employees other than to call in the fire brigade which was not appropriate in the circumstances. A claim in negligence also failed for the same reason.

Risk assessment

3.41   The basic principle is that an employer must consider whether his manual handling operation gives rise to a risk of injury and, if it does, he should carry out a detailed assessment of the operation in question to see what steps are required to reduce the risk of injury to the lowest level reasonably practical. Although there are many steps which an employer can take to reduce the risk of injury to the lowest level reasonably practicable, the most important points are that training on manual handling techniques

---

[81]   [2002] EWCA Civ 953

should be in place and an evaluation of whether or not the task can be replaced or made easier with equipment should also be carried out. A failure to carry out a risk assessment is a breach of the Regulations; however, this does not necessarily mean that liability will be established, as the question of causation will still have to be considered. The appropriate question to consider is: what would the employer have done had it carried out a risk assessment and what steps would it have taken to reduce the risk of injury to the lowest level reasonably practicable?

3.42   If the manual handing operation does give rise to a risk of injury then a risk assessment should be carried out to see what steps the employer needs to take to reduce that risk to the lowest level reasonably practicable. The risk assessment filter in Appendix 3 of the Guidance Notes to the Regulations is helpful and the courts frequently lay great emphasis on these guidance notes. Finally, even if a risk assessment has not been carried out, the claimant still needs to prove that if one had been done steps would have been taken to reduce the risk. *Koonjul v Thameslink Healthcare Services*[82] was such a case, where no risk assessment had been carried out, yet the claimant failed. The case involved a care assistant at a care home who alleged that she injured her back when making a bed that was 18 inches off the ground. Hale LJ considered that assessing the risk of injury needs an element of realism and the context was important. This was a small care home with a small number of employees doing everyday tasks. Although some risk of injury could have been envisaged it was understandable why the bed had been placed against the wall. The defendant could have told the claimant to kneel down when making the bed, but Hale LJ commented:

If one again looks at it in the context of this particular employment, it is an employment involving a number of

---

[82]   [2000] PIQR 123

everyday tasks, any one of which could involve something which could be described as a manual handling operation - lifting bedding, moving beds around in order to make them, moving the chests of drawers, or moving the chair in order to make the bed. There are innumerable tasks around such a home, and the idea that the level of risk involved (which I have already said was very low) should be met by a precise evaluation of each of those tasks and precise warnings to each employee as to how each was to be carried out, seems to me to take the matter way beyond the realms of practicability.

3.43   In *Spencer v Boots The Chemist Ltd[83]*, the claimant, a dispensing chemist, claimed a repetitive strain injury resulting from reaching up to a shelf for dispensing bottles. Although the defendant had not carried out a risk assessment, the claim was dismissed. Although a risk assessment might have considered the claimants 'workstation' less than ideal, nevertheless any risks involved were not risks of such a nature that it was incumbent on any reasonably careful employer to take steps to counter or which were likely to lead in any reasonably foreseeable way to injury of the kind suffered if they were not taken.

3.44   The case of *Alsop v Sheffield City Council[84]*, is another case illustrating the Court of Appeal's 'common sense' approach. The claimant was a dustbin man employed by the defendant and was pulling a wheely-bin up a very steep concrete ramp when he slipped and fell. The trial judge dismissed the claim on the basis that there was no risk of injury in carrying out the task. Mantell LJ went further and said:

It seems to me also that even if it had been the judge's view that the risk was such as to involve the assessment of the operation of the City Council, and had such an assessment

---

[83]   [2002] EWCA Civ 1691, [2002] 2 All ER (D) 465 (Oct)
[84]   [2000] EWCA Civ 429

taken place there would have been nothing more for the City Council to do other than to inform its operatives to use their common sense when moving wheely-bins from one place to another. That would involve, in circumstances such as occurred in this case, the operative judging for himself the weight of the bin, the weather conditions and his own general fitness, as to whether or not it was appropriate to try to pull the wheely-bin up the slope or whether or not it would be better to make use of the steps or even, in certain circumstances, to take the wheely-bin to the end of the sloping section.

Training

3.45   It will be seen that reg 4(1)(b)(iii) calls for employers to take appropriate steps by way of training. In *Koonjul v Thameslink Healthcare Services*[85], a care assistant at a care home for children allegedly injured her back when making a bed. The bed was a child's bed and was some 18 inches off the ground. As has been seen already in para 3.42 above, although no risk assessment had been carried out, nevertheless the claimant failed because the task which she was carrying out was so mundane that the Court of Appeal did not consider that any person in her position needed training in, or instructions on, how to make the bed.

3.46   The question of training and causation arose in *Warner v Huntingdonshire District Council.*[86] As has been said, training is one method of reducing the risk of injury to the lowest level reasonably practicable. If training has not been provided, it is relatively easy to find a breach, but it is still necessary to consider whether the breach caused the accident. The failure to train a dustbin man in carrying sacks was not causative of the injury since it had not been shown

---

[85]   [2000] PIQR 123
[86]   [2002] EWCA Civ 791

that training would have made any practical difference to the way in which the claimant went about his work.

3.47   On the other hand, in *O'Neill v DSG Retail*[87], the claimant was carrying a microwave oven when a colleague called out and he turned around instinctively, injuring his back. The defendant had carried out a risk assessment which stated that products between 10kg and 20kg 'may present a hazard if held away from the body, from excessive twisting of trunk, overstretching or lifting on steps or slopes'. It further said that 'all staff have to be trained to understand and observe good handling techniques wherever possible. In particular staff should understand the effects of the following twisting the body while supporting a load ...'. The defendant also had a training programme which included a video showing instances designed to reduce instinctive responses. The claimant had not been given any training and had not seen the video. The Court of Appeal took the view that if he had received training the claimant would have understood the risks involved in twisting his body whilst carrying a load. There was a foreseeable risk of injury present and this view was reinforced by the inclusion in the video of instances showing instinctive response. Nelson J, sitting in the Court of Appeal, said:

> *The submission of the defendant that the "appropriate level" of training could not include the 'training out' of instinctive responses cannot be correct. The obligation under the regulations is to "reduce the risk of injury", not to eliminate the risk of injury.*

3.48   In contrast with *Koonjul* this was not the carrying out of an everyday task because the defendant had recognised the need to increase its employees' awareness of the risks.

---

[87]   [2002] EWCA Civ 1139, [2003] ICR 223

Equipment

3.49   At common law the employer has a duty to take reasonable
        care to select the right equipment for the employee's tasks
        and to provide and maintain that equipment. Regular
        inspections will be required, as will repairs and maintenance
        as and when necessary.

The Provision and Use of Work Equipment Regulations 1998

3.50   The Provision and Use of Work Equipment Regulations
        1998 are the chief regulations relating to the supply of
        suitable and properly maintained work equipment. They
        repealed and replaced a large number of older regulations
        relating to specific pieces of equipment. The 1992 version of
        these regulations was considered by the Court of Appeal in
        Stark v Post Office[88]. Regulation 6(1) states:

> *Every employer shall ensure that work equipment is
> maintained in an efficient state, in efficient working order
> and in good repair.*

3.51   The claimant was injured when the bicycle which he had
        been given by his employer for the purposes of his work
        stopped suddenly because part of the front brake broke in
        two and lodged in the front wheel. The accident was not
        foreseeable in the sense that an inspection of the bicycle
        immediately before the accident would not have revealed the
        defect. The Court of Appeal held that there was nonetheless
        liability under reg 6(1) since it imposed on the employer an
        absolute obligation to provide work equipment which was in
        good working order. The situation is, it seems, to be judged
        immediately before the accident rather than at the time the
        work equipment was first supplied. The Court of Appeal
        accepted that the Directive pursuant to which the
        Regulations were made did not require any such absolute

---

[88]   [2000] 1 CR 1013, [2000] PIQR P 105

obligation. It held, however, that the Directive laid down minimum standards and that Parliament was entitled to go beyond those.

3.52   Regulation 5(1) of the 1998 Regulations was considered in *Ball v Street*[89]. The claimant was using a baling machine owned by the defendant when he was injured by a broken spring. The defendant argued (relying on *Fytche v Wincanton Logistics plc* – see paragraph 3.61 below) that the duty to repair and maintain applied only to an item's suitability as work equipment. He argued that the machine was still fit for its task even after the spring broke and further that this had been an "unforeseeable freak accident". The Court of Appeal preferred to follow *Stark* and also explained that the focus of the Regulations was on the general consideration of safety. Potter LJ said:

The focus of the 1998 Regulations is not upon the identification and assessment of risk for the purpose of providing safety equipment suitable for protection against a particular risk or hazard identified and not controlled by other means; it is upon general considerations of safety against the broad risk of accidental injury inherent in the use of machinery which is not maintained in good repair and efficient working order.

Work Equipment

3.53   Whether an item falls within the definition of "work equipment" has been the subject of a number of decisions. The relevant part of the 1998 Regulations is as follows:

2(1)   *Work Equipment means any machinery, appliance, apparatus, tool or installation for use at work (whether exclusively or not).*

---

[89]   [2005] EWCA Civ 76

> 3(2) *The requirements imposed by these Regulations on an employer in respect of work equipment shall apply to such equipment provided for use or used by an employer if he is at work.*

3.54 In *Hammond v Commissioner of Police for the Metropolis*[90] the claimant, employed by the defendant was injured when a wheel bolt sheared off a police vehicle which he was repairing. The vehicle was owned by the Metropolitan Police Authority. The Court of Appeal considered that the regulations did not apply to something which the employer was working on, but which had been provided by others. Thus, the vehicle that had been taken to the garage for repair was not owned by the defendant and although it might be "work equipment" of the policeman driving it, it was not "work equipment" of the police mechanic repairing the vehicle. The decision in *Hammond* was, however, disapproved by the House of Lords in *Spencer-Franks v Kellog Brown and Root Limited*[91].

3.55 In *Spencer-Franks* the claimant was injured while repairing a "door closer". A screw became loose and the linkage arm struck the claimant in the face. Lord Hoffmann noted the words in Regulation 2(1), "for use at work" and considered that the position was clear:

Everyone using the control room was using it for the purposes of their work. They used the door to enter or leave the control room. And, in doing so, they used the closer. Its purpose was for use at work. Giving the definition its ordinary meaning, the closer was work equipment.

Lord Hoffmann considered that the Court of Appeal had been wrong in *Hammond* when it decided that the vehicle might be the work equipment of a policeman but not of the

[90]   [2004] EWCA Civ 830, [2004] ICR 1467
[91]   [2008] UKHL 46

police mechanic repairing it. He considered that it was first necessary to decide whether the apparatus was work equipment, and then to decide if the Regulations applied to the equipment. The vehicle in *Hammond* was "for use at work" under Regulation 2(1) of the 1998 Regulations and it was therefore work equipment.

3.56   Lord Hoffmann noted that the Court of Appeal in *Hammond* had been concerned by the possibility that if a car brought to a garage for repair was regarded as work equipment in relation to a mechanic employed by the garage, his employer would be strictly liable for defects in the car, over which he could have no possible control. Although Lord Hoffmann did not give a decision on this point, he made it clear that he would regard it as a "strange result" if such a third party's car was covered by the regulations. He considered that while such a car might be "work equipment", it would not have been "made available to workers in the undertaking and/or establishment". This raises issues under Regulation 3(2) of the 1998 Regulations which has also been considered by the House of Lords (see para 3.58 below).

3.57   In *PRP Architects v Precious Reid*[92] the claimant was using a lift when leaving work and was injured when the lift door closed on her hand. It was argued that the 1998 Regulations did not apply because the lift had not been provided for the claimant's use by the defendant's employer, however, the Court of Appeal considered that the claimant, when leaving her office at the end of the day's work, and using a lift located in the lobby of a building where she worked, was "using the lift at work" for the purpose of Regulation 3(2). It was not appropriate to draw a line either when the claimant left the office to enter the lift or when the lift left the office floor. Accordingly, the employer was liable for the accident.

---

[92]   [2006] EWCA Civ 1119

3.58   Regulation 3(2) of the 1998 Regulations has now been considered by the House of Lords in *Smith v Northamptonshire County Council*[93] the claimant was employed as a carer/driver by the defendant Local Authority. As part of her duties, she was required to collect a lady from her home in her wheelchair and take her by minibus to a day centre. As the claimant was pushing the wheelchair down a ramp leading out of the house, the edge of the ramp gave way causing her to stumble and injure herself. The ramp had been installed originally by the NHS. It had been inspected by the defendant, but the defect was latent and not discoverable on inspection. Thus, a claim in common law negligence would have failed. Following *Spencer-Franks*, it was conceded that the ramp was "work equipment" under Regulation 2(1). In considering the question of liability under Regulation 3(2), however, by a majority, the House of Lords held that there had to be a clear and specific connection between the work equipment and the employer's undertaking, which went further than the mere fact of use. Lord Neuberger considered that the question was whether the employer had "control over the equipment". On the facts of the case, the defendant had not provided the ramp, did not own the ramp, nor did it have any responsibility or right to repair it.

3.59   The question of control was considered by the Court of Appeal in *Mason v Satelcom Ltd and East Potential Limited*[94]. The case was concerned with Regulation 3(3) of the 1998 Regulations which apply the Regulations "to a person who has control to any extent of work equipment and to the extent of his control". The claimant was injured when he fell from a ladder whilst working in a building owned by East Potential Limited. The issue was whether East Potential Limited had control over the ladder for the purpose of Regulation 3(3). There was no evidence present to show to

---

[93]   [2009] UKHL 27
[94]   [2008] EWCA Civ 494

whom the ladder belonged. Because East Potential Limited could have removed the ladder from the room in which it was located, it had control over the ladder and could stop it getting in anyone's way, but that was the limited extent of the control. The Court of Appeal considered that it would be "absurd" to hold that East Potential Limited had imposed on it the various obligations relating to suitability, maintenance, training and inspection just because the ladder happened to be on their premises.

Training

3.60   In *Allison v London Underground Limited*[95] the Court of Appeal considered the issue of training under the 1998 Regulations. The claimant, an underground train driver, developed tenosynovitis by her constant holding of the brake controller. No special instructions had been given to underground drivers as to how they should position their thumb on the brake controller. Under Regulation 9 of the 1998 Regulations, the duty to provide training is mandatory, however, the Court of Appeal did not consider that this introduced no-fault liability, as this would require clear wording. The "adequacy" of the training was to be judged in the light of what the employer ought to have known about the risks arising from his business. This meant that an employer must investigate the risks inherent in his operations, taking professional advice where necessary. It was not enough for the training to deal with risks about which the employer knew already. The defendants should have obtained advice from a suitable expert before putting the new brake controller into service. Had this happened, the advice would have identified the need for drivers to be trained in the use of the brake controller.

---

[95] [2008] EWCA Civ 71

Other Provisions relating to equipment

3.61   Personal safety equipment is regulated by the Personal Protective Equipment at Work Regulations 1992, which require an employer to 'ensure that suitable personal protective equipment is provided' to employees who may be exposed to risks, except where the risk is adequately controlled by other means. The protective equipment supplied must be properly maintained. The scope of the duty to maintain was considered by the House of Lords in *Fytche v Wincanton Logistics*[96]. A driver was given steel-capped safety boots to protect against injury from heavy objects. One boot developed a small hole which led to frostbite. By majority, the House of Lords held that there was no breach of the duty to maintain equipment in good repair because the defect was irrelevant to the function of the boots for the safety purposes for which they were supplied.

3.62   Additional protection for employees in relation to defects in equipment is provided by the Employers' Liability (Defective Equipment) Act 1969. Section 1 of the Act reads:

(1)   *Where, after the commencement of this Act:*

    (a)   *An employee suffers personal injury in the course of his employment in consequence of a defect in equipment provided by his employer for the purposes of the employer's business; and*

    (b)   *The defect is attributable wholly or partly to the fault of a third party (whether identified or not),*

(2)   The injury shall be deemed to be also attributable to negligence on the part of the employer.

---

[96]   [2004] UKHL 31, [2004] ICR 975

3.63   This Act was passed as a result of the decision of the House of Lords in *Davie v New Merton Board Mills Ltd*[97], where a workman was injured when using a defective tool supplied to him by his employer. The tool had been manufactured negligently by reputable manufacturers and no reasonable inspection by the employer would have revealed the defect. The action failed on the basis that the employer had discharged its duty to provide safe equipment to the employee by purchasing the tool from a reputable manufacturer. As a result of the Act, an employer is now able to defend such a claim on the basis that the defect was caused by negligence of another such as the manufacturer or supplier of equipment. In any event, under the Provision and Use of Work Equipment Regulations 1998 the obligation to provide efficient work equipment is absolute (see para 3.50 above).

Stress in the workplace

3.64   It is well established in law that an employer is under a duty to ensure the safety of its employees' physical and mental well-being whilst at work. The first 'stress' case to reach the appeal level in the United Kingdom was *Petch v Commissioners of Customs & Excise*[98]. The claimant was a civil servant who suffered a mental breakdown at work. Although he was unsuccessful in establishing liability on appeal, the Court of Appeal did confirm that there was no reason why claimants could not claim for mental illness as opposed to physical injury.

3.65   Although, strictly speaking, the case did not establish anything new, *Walker v Northumberland County Council*[99] was the first successful claim by an employee who alleged

---

[97]   [1959] AC 604
[98]   [1993] ICR 789
[99]   [1995] 1 All ER 737

that he was suffering from a psychiatric illness resulting from pressure of work. The claimant was a senior social worker with the council. He had a period off work, which the council knew was the result of a depressive illness brought on by stress at work. The council agreed to take steps to lighten the load on the claimant's return to work. However, in fact, it did nothing and, as a result, the claimant suffered another breakdown. He never returned to work. The important feature of all cases relating to workplace stress is that of 'foreseeability'. The judge held that the council was not liable for the first depressive illness because it could not have reasonably foreseen the illness; however, the Council was liable for the second depressive illness because by that time the council knew about the claimant's problem.

3.66   Dealing with the duty of care, Coleman J said:

Where it was reasonably foreseeable to an employer that an employee might suffer a nervous breakdown because of the stress and pressures of his workload, the employer was under a duty of care, as part of the duty to provide a safe system of work, not to cause the employee psychiatric damage by reason of the volume or character of the work which the employee was required to perform.

3.67   There have been a number of similar workplace 'stress' claims since *Walker,* many in the public sector, and as a result, in 2002 the Court of Appeal felt it appropriate to give general guidance in a series of four appeals which they heard together under the name *Sutherland v Hatton*[100]. The Court of Appeal emphasised a number of points as follows:

(i)   The crucial question is whether this kind of harm to this particular employee was reasonably foreseeable. Relevant factors on the issue of foreseeability include:

---

[100]   [2002] EWCA Ci 76, [2002] 2 All ER 1

- The nature and extent of the work done by the employee.
- Is the workload much more than is normal for a particular job?
- Are there signs that others doing this job are suffering harmful levels of stress?
- Is there an abnormal level of sickness or absenteeism in the same job or same department?
- Has the individual a particular problem or vulnerability?
- Has he already suffered from illness attributable to stress at work?
- Have there recently been frequent or prolonged absences which are uncharacteristic?
- An employer is generally entitled to take what it is told by its employee at face value. It does not generally have to make searching inquiries of the employee or seek permission to make further inquiries of its medical advisors.
- Indications of impending harm to health arising from stress at work must be plain enough for any reasonable employer to realise that it should do something about it.
- There are no occupations which should be regarded as intrinsically dangerous to mental health.

(ii)   An employer is only in breach of duty of it fails to take steps which are reasonable in the circumstances, bearing in mind the magnitude of the risk of harm occurring and the cost and practicability of preventing it.

(iii)   An employer can only reasonably be expected to take steps which are likely to do some good.

(iv)   An employer who offers a confidential advice service, with referral to appropriate counselling or treatment services, is unlikely to be found in breach of duty.

(v)   Where the harm suffered has more than one cause, the employer should only pay for that proportion of the harm suffered which is attributable to its wrongdoing.

3.68   The House of Lords approved the above guidance in *Barber v Somerset County Council*[101], however, they overruled the decision of the Court of Appeal on the facts *(Barber* was one of the four appeals heard by the Court of Appeal in *Sutherland v Hatton).* The claimant was a schoolteacher whose job involved increasing duties as a result of changes at the school. He had a period off work with depression and, on his return, told his head teacher about the problem. A few months later, the claimant suffered another breakdown at school and left. He did not return to work. The Court of Appeal had taken the view that the school could not foresee the second breakdown as it had followed the school's summer holiday, and the claimant had not told anyone that he was still seeing his GP with depression. However, the House of Lords took the view that the head teacher had been put on notice of the problem and should have taken steps to find out how the claimant was coping. Therefore, rather than simply relying on the view that an employer does not generally have to make searching inquiries of the employee, the House of Lords preferred the statement of general principle in *Stokes v Guest, Keen and Nettlefold (Bolt and Nuts) Ltd*[102] as follows:

The overall test is still the conduct of the reasonable and prudent employer, taking positive thought for the safety of its workers in the light of what he knows or ought to know ...

3.69   The Court of Appeal gave further guidance in a series of six

---

[101]   [2004] 1 WLR 1089, [2004] 1 All ER 385
[102]   [1968] 1 WLR 1776

cases heard together under the name *Hartman v South Essex Mental Health and Community Care NHS Trust*[103]. Once again the Court of Appeal confirmed that the guidance provided in *Sutherland v Hatton* remains appropriate; however, it stressed that the guidance was not intended to cover all circumstances. The Court of Appeal confirmed the importance of foreseeability in stress at work cases. The following points also arose:

- In *Hartman,* the fact that the claimant had disclosed to the employer's occupational health department relevant information about her medical history was not ordinarily knowledge to be imputed to the employer because the information was confidential (in contrast with the position under the Disability Discrimination Act 1995).

- Although in the case of *Best v Staffordshire University* there had been a memorandum from the claimant's supervisor pointing out that staff were generally overworked, this information was not specific to the claimant. The employer therefore could not be expected to foresee Mr Best's breakdown.

- In *Green v Grimsby & Scunthorpe Newspapers Ltd.,* the claimant had sent a memorandum to his employer expressing concern that his work was affecting his health, however, he walked out before giving the employer a chance to discuss the problem. The employer had no knowledge prior to the memorandum and therefore the claim failed.

- The case of *Wheeldon v HSBC Bank Ltd* is interesting in that it involves a part-time worker at a bank. The bank was well aware of Mrs Wheeldon's problems and her claim succeeded very much along the lines of *Walker v Northumberland*

---

[103]   [2005] IRLR 293, [2005] PIQR P19

68

County Council. Nevertheless, it confirms that a part-time worker can succeed in a claim for work-related stress.

- In *Moore v Welwyn Components Ltd* the appeal was concerned with the apportionment of damages where there is more than one cause of psychiatric illness. The claimant had a history of psychiatric illness and there were factors in his private life that gave rise to the claimant's medical problems. Although the claimant's general damages for pain and suffering were discounted to reflect the other causative factors, the loss of earnings claim was not discounted. The Court of Appeal stressed that it was for the defendant's employers to call medical evidence to establish the other relevant causative factors before the court would apportion the damages. In the absence of such evidence there could be no discount.

- The claimant in *Melville v The Home Office* was employed in a prison, one of his duties being the recovery of bodies of prisoners who had committed suicide. After one such incident the claimant alleged that he had developed a stress related illness. The Home Office had established a system to support such employees, but the prison involved did not implement the Home Office procedures. The claimant had given no prior indication of developing a stress-related illness before he stopped work. The Home Office therefore argued that his illness was not foreseeable. The Court of Appeal disagreed. The Home Office clearly had foreseen that employees such as the claimant could suffer a psychiatric injury as a result of their work with suicide victims. These were particularly traumatic events as a result of which psychiatric injury was foreseeable.

- It should be noted that the Court of Appeal was careful to point out that the mere fact that an employer had offered an occupational health service did not, of itself, mean that the employer had foreseen that psychiatric injury would occur.

The decision in *Sutherland v Hatton* was still correct when it said that an employer was unlikely to be in breach of duty if he offered a confidential advice service. Furthermore, even where an employer has assessed that there is some risk of psychiatric injury, it is still open to him to argue that the risk is so small that it is reasonable to neglect it.

3.70   It is clear from *Sutherland, Barber* and *Hartman* that foreseeability will generally be crucial when considering cases of psychiatric injury caused by stress at work. In *Pratley v Surrey County Council*[104] the claimant, shortly before going on holiday, complained to her supervisor about her workload and that she feared for her health in the future if nothing was done to reduce the workload. The supervisor promised to introduce a new system of working which would reduce the workload. On the claimant's return from holiday, she saw that the new system of working had not been introduced. She immediately suffered a breakdown and never returned to work. The Court of Appeal decided that although the supervisor was in a position to foresee the risk of illness through the continuing workload at some time in the future, nevertheless the claimant's immediate collapse on return from holiday was not foreseeable. According to Buxton LJ, the failure to introduce the new system as promised was potentially negligent if persisted in for the longer term:

But since the immediate collapse was neither foreseen, nor foreseeable, the failure to make immediate provision to prevent it could not be a relevant act of negligence.

3.71   *Pratley can* be contrasted with *Young v Post Office*[105], where the Court of Appeal considered that the psychiatric illness suffered by the claimant was foreseeable. The claimant had suffered a breakdown. He returned to work with the promise

---

[104]   [2004] ICR 159, [2004) PIQR P17
[105]   [2002] EWCA Civ 661, [2002] IRLR 660

that his workload would be limited and that indeed that he could stop work and go home if he could not cope. The claimant found the workload too much on his return, but did not complain. He then suffered another breakdown. The Court of Appeal considered that the second breakdown was foreseeable. The court also rejected an argument that the claimant had contributed to his injury by not complaining to his employer.

3.72   The position of an employer who offers a confidential counselling service (see *Sutherland*, para 3.67(vii) above) was considered by the Court of Appeal in *Daw v Intelcorp (UK) Limited*[106]. The claimant suffered a breakdown and on her return to work the defendants promised to provide her with an assistant, but this never happened. The claimant became depressed and was signed off work. In defending the claim, the defendant relied on the availability of a confidential counselling service to the claimant. The Court of Appeal held that injury to the claimant's health was foreseeable, at least after her initial breakdown. The Court of Appeal then went on to consider what the Court had said in *Sutherland* concerning the availability of counselling services. The judge had to consider the facts of each particular case. Although the availability of counselling services might provide a defence to some claims, the problem in this case was one which could only be dealt with by reducing the claimant's workload. The failure to take "urgent and appropriate action" was the cause of the severe depression. A similar decision is to be found in *Dickins v O2 Plc*[107]. The claimant told her employers that she was "stressed out" and wanted six months off work. The Court of Appeal considered that the employers had "received a clear indication of impending illness" and that the claimant's illness was foreseeable. Although the employers suggested that the claimant use their confidential counselling service,

---

[106]   [2007] EWCA Civ 70
[107]   [2008] EWCA Civ 1144

she did not do so. The Court of Appeal referred to *Daw* and Smith LJ said:

Given the situation where the claimant was describing severe symptoms alleging they were due to stress at work and was warning that she did not know for how long she could carry on, I do not think that a mere suggestion that she seek counselling could be regarded as an adequate response.

3.73   In *Dickins*, the Court of Appeal also considered the questions of causation and apportionment of damages. The claimant had a vulnerable personality and had problems at home. The Court of Appeal considered that the appropriate test for causation was whether the defendant's breach of duty made a "material contribution" to the claimant's illness. Although the claimant's vulnerable personality was an underlying cause of her breakdown, nevertheless the defendant's failure plainly made a material contribution. The Court of Appeal also considered, *obiter,* the apportionment of damages as referred to Hale LJ in *Sutherland* (see para 3.67 (viii) above). Following the decision in *Bailey v Ministry of Defence* [108], the Court of Appeal doubted that it was appropriate to apportion damages for stress-related psychiatric injury, although there could be a reduction in some heads of damage, for example future loss of earnings, to reflect a claimant's vulnerability to a psychiatric breakdown at some time in the future, even without the defendant's tort.

Nervous shock/post traumatic stress disorder

3.74   The duty of care not to cause someone to suffer physical injury, where the risk of physical injury is reasonably foreseeable, is a straightforward concept. In the case of psychiatric injury, however, the courts have, for policy reasons, restricted the circumstances in which liability arises for causing foreseeable psychiatric injury. It is an inevitable

---

[108]   [2008] EWCA Civ 883

part of the work performed by the emergency services that their employees will be subjected to circumstances which might cause nervous shock. It is clear that there is a duty on the part of employers to exercise reasonable care not to cause psychiatric injury by putting an employee in fear of his physical safety. The courts have, however, restricted the circumstances in which there can be a claim for psychiatric injury as a result of the defendant causing the death of someone ('the primary victim') which is witnessed by the claimant ('the secondary victim'). This is the case even where the claimant is employed by the defendant.

3.75 Whether police officers could recover for nervous shock/post-traumatic stress disorder as a result of witnessing disasters in the course of their duty was considered in the case of *White & Others v Chief Constable of South Yorkshire & Others*[109]. This case followed the disaster at the Hillsborough Football Stadium in 1989 when 95 people on the terraces were crushed to death and many more were injured. On that day the claimants were serving members of the South Yorkshire Police Force on duty at the stadium or elsewhere in Sheffield. Each became involved in the aftermath in some way or other. Two helped to carry the dead and dying. Two tried unsuccessfully to give resuscitation to those who had been laid out on the ground. One assisted at the hospital mortuary. The claimants suffered from post-traumatic stress disorder and the symptoms affected their ability to work and their private lives. They claimed damages in negligence against the Chief Constable of South Yorkshire and two other defendants. The claims for post-traumatic stress disorder brought by relatives of the victims had already been rejected by the House of Lords in the case of *Alcock v Chief Constable of South Yorkshire*[110]. The claimants in the case of *White* said that they were in a different position - they were analogous to employees of the

---

[109]   [1999] All ER 550
[110]   [1992] 1 AC 3l0

73

Chief Constable and could claim the employment relationship gave rise to duties which were not owed to strangers.

3.76   In *Page v Smith*[111] the House of Lords allowed a claim for "freestanding" psychiatric injury from the victim of a road accident who had, in fact, suffered no physical injury. In the case of such an accident victim, it was considered sufficient that injury, whether physical or psychiatric, could be foreseen. *Page* has been criticised and the House of Lords refused to extend the principle in *Johnstone v NEI International Combustion Limited*[112].

3.77   The House of Lords ruled that the police officers could not recover damages as employees or rescuers for psychiatric injury. A recognition of the claims would have substantially expanded the existing categories in which compensation could be recovered for pure psychiatric harm and would have sat uneasily with the denial of the claims of bereaved relatives in the case of *Alcock*.

Psychiatric injury as a result of disciplinary proceedings

3.78   Difficult issues arise where an employee claims damages for psychiatric injury caused by disciplinary procedures and/or the termination of employment. Following *Addis v Gramophone Co. Ltd.*[113], it is usually understood that damages for wrongful dismissal cannot include compensation for injured feelings for the manner of dismissal and so forth. As a result of employment protection legislation (at present chiefly contained in the Employment Rights Act 1996), Parliament has intervened to give a right to compensation for the manner of dismissal if it is unfair. In

---

[111]   [1996] 1 AC 155
[112]   [2007] UKHL 39
[113]   [1909] AC 488

Johnson v Unisys Ltd[114] the House of Lords had to consider whether a claimant who was rendered psychiatrically ill by the circumstances and manner of his dismissal had a right to compensation. The allegations were effectively that the employer had dismissed the claimant on the basis of ill-defined allegations, which were never properly put to the claimant and against which he had no right to defend himself. Among other complaints was a failure to implement the proper disciplinary procedure. The claimant brought a claim for unfair dismissal in the employment tribunal and won. He now sought to claim some £400,000 for the psychiatric damage that had been caused to him, basing the claim chiefly on breach of the implied obligation of trust and confidence. His claim was dismissed by the House of Lords. The Court of Appeal had similarly dismissed the claim. It had based its decision on the rule in *Addis*. The House of Lords, however, took a different route, indicating that it would probably not have felt constrained by *Addis*. The majority of their Lordships held that the crucial factor was that Parliament had legislated in this field to fill a perceived gap in the common law.

3.79   The scope of the rule in *Johnson* has not proved easy to define. In *Eastwood v Magnox Electric plc*[115] the House of Lords considered two cases. The first was brought by two employees who claimed to have suffered stress-related illnesses caused by an alleged campaign of harassment on the part of their employer before they were dismissed. After dismissal, both employees brought and settled unfair dismissal claims. The second case was a claim by a teacher suspended and dismissed for inappropriate behaviour towards a female pupil. He brought and succeeded on an unfair dismissal claim. In the claim before their Lordships, he claimed damages for failures in the investigation procedures which he said led to stress-related illness. The

---

[114]   [2001] 2 WLR 1076, [2001] 2 All ER 801
[115]   [2004] UKHL 35, [2004] 3 WLR 322

House of Lords refused to strike out either claim, stating that, on the assumed facts, it did not fall foul of the rule in *Johnson*. Lord Nicholls said:

Identifying the boundary of the Johnson "exclusion area", as it has been called, is comparatively straightforward. The statutory code provides remedies for infringement of the statutory right not to be dismissed unfairly. An employee's remedy for unfair dismissal, whether actual or constructive, is the remedy provided by statute. If before his dismissal, whether actual or constructive, an employee has acquired a cause of action at law, for breach of contract or otherwise, that cause of action remains unimpaired by his subsequent unfair dismissal and the statutory rights flowing there from. By definition, in law, such a cause of action exists independently of the dismissal.

3.80   Lord Steyn particularly pointed out that part of the chain of reasoning in *Johnson* was the view that damages for the distress caused by the manner of dismissal could be awarded in an unfair dismissal claim, and that this view had now been shown to be wrong by the decision of the House in *Dunnachie v Kingston Upon Hull City Council*[116].

3.81   An example in practice is *Deadman v Bristol City Council*[117] where the claimant was the subject of disciplinary proceedings following allegations against him of sexual harassment. The claimant became depressed because of the way in which the disciplinary proceedings were handled and he stopped work. The Court of Appeal held that there was no evidence that the defendant should have been aware that the claimant's health was liable to be affected by the ordinary operation of its procedure of investigating complaints. Although, in fact, the procedure was not followed precisely, nevertheless it was not reasonably foreseeable that this

---

[116] [2004] 3 WLR 310
[117] [2007] EWCA Civ 822

would affect the claimant. This followed the decision in
Barber v Somerset County Council [118] (see para 3.69 above).

3.82   In considering this area generally, one should have regard to
        the Disability Discrimination Act 1995. In appropriate cases
        a claimant can use that Act to seek compensation avoiding
        difficult issues as to whether injuries or feelings alone should
        be compensated.

Harassment

3.83   The decision in *Lister v Hesley Hall Ltd*[119] has made it more
        difficult for employers to defend bullying and harassment
        claims on the grounds that the employee's behaviour went
        outside the course of his employment.

3.84   Where the harassment is of a sexual or racial kind, and is
        committed in the course of employment, an employer will be
        liable unless it has done all that was reasonably practicable
        to prevent it[120]. Where an employee suffers from harassment
        of a sexual or racial kind, it is not necessary to prove
        psychiatric illness. Injury to feelings will suffice[121].

3.85   The question of harassment was considered in *Banks v Ablex
        Ltd.*[122] where the claimant alleged that a fellow employee
        had been grossly aggressive and abusive and had put her in
        fear that he was going to strike her. As a result she left her
        employment and was found subsequently to be suffering
        from a depressive disorder of modest severity which
        rendered her unfit for work. The defendant company denied
        that the claimant had complained about any prior incident
        involving the fellow employee. The claim was brought under

---

[118]   [2004] 1 WLR 1089, [2004] 1 All ER 385
[119]   [2001] UKHL 22, [2002] IAC 215
[120]   Sex Discrimination Act 1975, S 41; Race Relations Act 1976, S 32
[121]   Sex Discrimination Act 1975, ss 65-66; Race Relations Act 1976, ss 56-57
[122]   [2005] IRLR 357

the Protection from Harassment Act 1997. The Court of Appeal concluded that the tort of harassment was not complete unless the conduct of the alleged tort was intentional and was directed at another person on more than one occasion, knowing that it would cause harassment to that person. An employer could be neither in breach of its contractual duty to provide a safe system of work nor vicariously liable for abusive and aggressive behaviour of a male employee towards a female employee at their place of work when the requirements of the tort were not proved.

3.86 The Protection from Harassment Act 1997 has now been considered by the House of Lords in *Majrowski v Guy's & St Thomas NHS Trust*[123]. The claimant brought proceedings under Section 3 of the Protection from Harassment Act 1997 for distress and anxiety and consequential losses caused by harassment by his departmental manager. Section 3 provides:

(1) *An actual or apprehended breach of Section 1 may be the subject of a claim in civil proceedings by the person who is or may be the victim of the course of conduct in question.*

(2) *On such a claim, damages may be awarded for (among other things) any anxiety caused by the harassment and any financial loss resulting from the harassment.*

3.87 The claim against the defendant was limited to one of vicarious liability whereby it was alleged that the claimant's line manager had been acting in the course of her employment. The question for the House of Lords was whether the Protection from Harassment Act gives rise to a claim in vicarious liability against an employer for the acts of its employees.

---

[123] [2006] UKHL 34

3.88   Lord Nicholls saw no reason to confine vicarious liability to common law wrongs. As a general principle, he said:

> *Does employer's vicarious liability arise <u>unless</u> the statutory provision expressly or impliedly <u>excludes</u> such liability? Or does employer's liability arise only if the statutory provision expressly or impliedly <u>envisages</u> such liability may arise? As already indicated, I prefer the first alternative. It is more consistent with the general rule that employers are liable for wrongs committed by employees in the course of their employment. The general rule should apply in respect of wrongs having a statutory source unless the statute displaces the ordinary rule.*

3.89   The defendants argued that the Act was not aimed at the workplace. It was a public order provision designed to punish perpetrators for the anxiety and upset caused to victims, and not blameless employers who happened to be solvent and available as a target for litigation. The House of Lords did not agree. They considered that 124 Section 3 had created a new cause of action, a new civil wrong. Lord Nicholls said:

> *The effect of Section 3(1) is to render a breach of Section 1, a wrong giving rise to the ordinary remedies the law provides for civil wrongs. This includes an entitlement to damages for any loss or damage sustained by a victim by reason of the wrongs. Ordinary principles of causation and mitigation and the like apply vicarious liability, arising only if the new wrong is committed by an employee in the course of his employment, as already described. The act of the employee must meet the 'close connection' test. If an employee's acts of harassment meet this test, I am at a loss to see why these particular features of this newly created wrong should be thought to place this wrong in a special category in which an employer is exempt from vicarious liability. It is true that this new wrong usually comprises conduct of an intensely personal character between two*

individuals. But this feature may also be present with other wrongs which attract vicarious liability, such as assault.

3.90   Although the decision of the House of Lords was unanimous, it seems clear that, apart from Lord Nicholls, their Lordships considered that there were "powerful reasons" or thinking that Parliament intended that liability and damages should be personal to the perpetrator of the harassment and that it should not be extended to his employer, however, looking at the statute as a whole, their Lordships were all agreed that, in fact, the statute did allow claims in vicarious liability.

3.91   In *Daniels v Commissioner of Police for the Metropolis*[124], the Court confirmed that a claim under the Protection from Harassment Act 1997 requires a course of conduct of at least two occasions of harassment, although the course of conduct could be either that of one employee or more than one employee. On the facts, the claim in *Daniels* failed. Similarly, in *Conn v The Council and City of Sunderland*[125], the claimant also failed to establish two incidents of harassment. The Court pointed out that a civil claim under the Act is only available as a remedy for a breach of Section 1 of the Act which, by Section 2, means a criminal offence. Gage LJ said:

It seems to me that what, in the words of Lord Nicholls in Majrowski, crosses the boundary between unattractive and even unreasonable conduct and conduct which is oppressive and unacceptable, may well depend on the context in which the conduct occurred. What might not be harassment on the factory floor or in the barrack room might well be harassment in the hospital ward and vice versa. In my judgment the touchstone for recognizing what is not harassment for the purposes of Sections 1 and 3 will be whether the conduct is of such gravity as to justify the sanctions of the criminal law.

---

[124]   [2006] EWHC 1622 (QB)
[125]   [2007] EWCA Civ 1492

Contributory negligence

3.92   If a court decides that although a defendant was in breach of duty, the claimant's own negligence contributed to the damage alleged, it must apportion the damage according to the degree of fault on both sides. Contributory negligence applies not only where the claimant's fault has contributed to the allegedly negligent incident, but also where the claimant's fault has affected the amount of loss or extent of injuries suffered. Therefore, in the case of a road traffic accident, a passenger who is injured when not wearing a seatbelt will have his damages reduced. On the other hand, if his injuries were not connected with the wearing of a seatbelt then there would be no reduction in damages.

3.93   In the context of employer's liability, courts have sometimes considered whether there should be a finding of contributory negligence in a claim based on breach of statutory duty and, if so, the extent of the apportionment. In *Toole v Bolton Metropolitan Borough Council*[126] the claimant suffered a needle stick injury when picking up a syringe. The claimant could not find the gloves which had been provided by his employer and accordingly he used rubber gloves to pick up the syringe. The judge found that even the gloves provided by the employer would not have given protection and, as a result, the employer was liable for failing to supply adequate equipment. Nevertheless the judge assessed the claimant's contributory negligence at 75%. The Court of Appeal noted that this was a case of breach of statutory duty and Buxton LJ said:

> *It is not usual for there to be marked findings of contributory negligence in a breach of statutory duty case.*

---

[126]   [2002] EWCA Civ 588

3.94   In the circumstances of the case the Court of Appeal overruled the decision on contributory negligence and the claimant recovered his damages in full.

3.95   In *Sherlock v Chester City Council*[127] the claimant was injured while using a circular saw. On appeal his claim succeeded on the basis that a risk assessment would have resulted in the provision of a relevant safety device. There was a breach of reg 4 of the Manual Handling Regulations 1992 and reg 8 of the Provision and Use of Work Equipment Regulations 1998 in that no instruction had been given to the claimant in the use of the saw. Dealing with contributory negligence, the Court of Appeal noted Buxton LJ's comment in *Toole,* but considered that here, the claimant's degree of fault was sufficient to merit an award of 60% contributory negligence.

---

[127]   [2004] EWCA Civ 201

FOUR

INDUSTRIAL DISEASE

Asbestos - mesothelioma

History

4.1   The first recorded fatal case of lung fibrosis in an asbestos worker in the UK was described by Dr H Montagu Murray in his evidence to a Home Office Departmental Committee on compensation on industrial diseases in 1907. The death had occurred in 1900. Apparently, the victim had told Dr Murray that he was the last surviving member of his workplace.

4.2   In 1930, the Merewether report outlined the effects of asbestos dust on the lungs, and dust suppression in the asbestos dust industry. The report demonstrated the link between chronic exposure to asbestos dust and the development of asbestosis. It recognised that 83 workers were likely to be exposed to dust containing asbestos in various industries involved in the insulation of boilers, pipes, and engines.

4.3   The Workmen's Compensation (Silicosis and Asbestosis) Act 1930 added asbestosis to the list of compensatable occupational diseases. This was followed by the Asbestosis Industry Regulations 1931[128] which came into force on 1 March 1932.

---

[128]   SI 1931/1140

Knowledge

4.4   By and large it is difficult to argue, particularly in cases involving heavy industry, that employers had no relevant knowledge about the risks associated with asbestos after 1931. It should be noted that a claimant need show only that the employer should have foreseen the risk of some pulmonary injury. It is not necessary to show that the employer should have foreseen mesothelioma.

4.5   In *Margereson v J W Roberts Ltd*[129] the Court of Appeal decided in favour of claimants who had been contaminated by asbestos while living near to the defendant's factory in the 1930s. The Merewether report was used as evidence of the date of knowledge applicable to the defendants.

4.6   In *Cherry Tree Machine Co. Ltd* and *Shell UK Ltd v Dawson and Jeromson*[130] the first claimant had been an apprentice fitter with Cherry Tree. The Court of Appeal confirmed that the Asbestos Regulations 1931 applied to the defendants. The regulations did not apply simply to the "asbestos industry" in the sense of employers whose business was the production of asbestos or asbestos products.

4.7   In response to Shell's appeal, which was concerned with events in the 1950s, the Court of Appeal considered that a reasonable and careful employer, taking positive thought for the safety of his employees, would at that time have identified the risk so that he took precautions, or at least sought advice as to what to do. Only if he could be reassured that none of his employees would be sufficiently exposed to be at risk, could he safely ignore the problem. In all the circumstances, the judge had been correct to approach breach of duty by looking into the potential exposure as

---

[129]   [1996] PIQR P358
[130]   [2001] PIQR P265

opposed to the <u>average</u> exposure of a marine engineer employed by Shell. There was knowledge of the risk of exposure in the 1950s. The fact that knowledge of <u>graver</u> risks came later did not detract from the relevance of what was already known at the material time, namely the 1950s, particularly as it affected employees such as the claimant working in confined spaces containing a great deal of asbestos which might be disturbed at any time. *Jeromson* was distinguished in *Abraham v G Ireson (Properties) Limited*[131] and another. The claimant was exposed to asbestos by his use of asbestos pads and string between 1956 and 1965. Considering whether the defendant should have identified the risk from exposure to asbestos, the court distinguished *Jeromson* on the basis that in that case there had been significant exposure to asbestos. In *Abraham*, given the claimant's infrequent use of asbestos, Swift J concluded it "highly unlikely" that an employer, on the basis of literature then available, and in the absence of any special knowledge, would have foreseen that he was exposing the employee to the risk of an asbestos related injury. Only after the publication of further literature in October 1965[132] could employers have anticipated the risk of exposure to asbestos at the low levels in this case.

Cause of action

4.8   It is a well-established principle in English law that a cause of action does not arise simply on the occurrence of negligence. There must be damage, and although such damage need not be substantial, it must be more than minimal. In the case of most industrial injuries, for example mesothelioma, the issue of the existence of injury gives rise to no difficulty. Although limitation might give rise to a

---

[131]   [2009] EWHC 1958 (QB)

[132]   Epidemiology of Pleural Peritoneum following exposure to Asbestos in the London area by Newhouse and Thompson, published in the Baker Journal of Industrial Medicine.

problem, in fact this has been avoided by the Limitation Act 1980 (see 4.25 below).

4.9   Where injury caused by negligence carries with it the chance that a claimant will suffer further physical damage in the future, the general damages recoverable by way of a final award will be increased to reflect the chance of this adverse outcome, however, no claim can be made in respect of the chance of contracting a future disease if it is not consequent upon some physical injury. Similarly, where there is physical injury, the Courts can make an award of general damages to reflect anxiety about what might happen in the future. On the other hand, there can be no freestanding claim for anxiety in the absence of physical injury.

Pleural Plaques

4.10   The above-mentioned principals were considered by the House of Lords in relation to pleural plaques in *Johnstone v NEI International Combustion Limited*[133]. The question for their Lordships was whether a claimant with pleural plaques has a cause of action on the basis, as was accepted, that pleural plaques are not in themselves harmful, do not threaten or lead to other asbestos induced conditions, and are not a necessary pre-condition for such conditions.

4.11   There had been a line of cases in the mid 1980's[134] which had decided that claimants with pleural plaques did have a cause of action. This appeared to be accepted thereafter by employers and insurers. In *Johnstone*, the House of Lords was in no doubt, that, taken by themselves, pleural plaques could not give rise to a cause of action. Save in the most exceptional cases, the plaques would never cause any symptoms, did not increase the susceptibility of the

---

[133] [2007] UKHL 39 (usually cited as "*Rothwell*")
[134] *Church v Ministry of Defence* [1983], *Sykes v Ministry of Defence* [1984] and *Patterson v Ministry of Defence* [1986]

claimants to other diseases, or shorten their expectation of life. They had no effect on a claimant's health at all.

4.12   The claimants argued that pleural plaques, when "aggregated" with the risk of future disease and anxiety, could give rise to a cause of action. There is no doubt that <u>if</u> a claimant does have a cause of action, he may recover damages for the risk that he may suffer further in consequence of the same act of negligence. He may also be able to recover damages for anxiety, consequent upon an actionable injury. The House of Lords stressed, however, that recovery of damages for this risk and anxiety is entirely dependant upon the <u>existence of an actionable injury</u>. The claimants' cases failed because such risk and anxiety are not to be taken into account in deciding <u>whether</u> the claimant has a cause of action.

Free-standing Psychiatric Illness

4.13   In one of the cases before the House of Lords in *Johnstone*, the claimant produced evidence that he had suffered a recognised psychiatric illness after being told that his pleural plaques indicated that he had had a significant exposure to asbestos. Did this give rise to a cause of action? The House of Lords relied upon the judgment of the Court of Appeal in *Hatton v Sutherland*[135], and confirmed that the question was whether this kind of psychiatric harm to this particular employee was reasonably foreseeable. In the absence of knowledge of a particular vulnerability in an employee, the employer is entitled to assume that his employees are persons of ordinary fortitude. Because an employer would be unlikely to have any specific knowledge of how a particular employee was likely to react to the risk of an asbestos-related illness, many years after leaving his employment, an assumption of ordinary fortitude was inevitable, and hence the claim failed for lack of foreseeability.

---

[135]   [2002] EWCA Civ 76, [2002] 2 All ER 1

Pleural Plaques – Legislation

4.14   Shortly after the decision in *Johnstone*, the government came under pressure to introduce legislation to reverse the effect of the House of Lords decision. To date the government in Westminster has not introduced legislation, indicating that it may prefer the alternative of a compensation scheme which would compensate at least some persons diagnosed with pleural plaques. At the same time, however, private members bills seeking to overturn the decision in *Johnstone* were introduced in both the House of Commons and the House of Lords in December 2009. In Scotland, the Scottish Parliament passed the Damages (Asbestos-Related Conditions)(Scotland) Act 2009 which overturned the ruling in *Johnstone* and declared that:

1.   Pleural Plaques

(1)   Asbestos-related Pleural Plaques are a personal injury which is not negligible.

(2)   Accordingly, they constitute actionable harm for the purposes of an action of damages for personal injuries.

The Scottish Act faced a challenge from insurance companies by way of judicial review under the Human Rights Act 1998 on the basis that the Act violated one or more of the rights set out in the European Convention on Human Rights. The Outer House, Court of Session, ruled against the insurance companies' challenge to the Act[136], but an appeal is pending.

Asbestosis

4.15   In considering whether asbestosis gives rise to a cause of

---

[136]   *Axa General Insurance Limited and Others, Judicial Review of the Damages (Asbestos-related conditions) (Scotland) Act 2009* [2010] CSOH 2

action the condition must have some perceptible effect albeit this necessarily equates to presence of clear symptoms. If a medical examination can identify an effect upon the claimant before he is aware of a symptom, then it can amount to damage provided it is more than minimal. In Scotland, however, Section 2 of the Damages (Asbestos – related conditions)(Scotland) Act 2009 provides that asbestosis, even when not causing impairment of a person's physical condition, is a personal injury which is not negligible.

Mesothelioma - causation

4.16   Where a claimant has worked for a number of employers (including periods of self-employment), on each occasion being exposed to asbestos dust, and he has contracted mesothelioma, the current state of scientific knowledge does not provide enough certainty to enable the claimant to establish which employment caused the mesothelioma. It is understood that mesothelioma can be caused by ingesting one fibre of asbestos and it is not, at present, possible to establish when this occurred in cases involving several employers where asbestos could have been encountered. Under the traditional approach to causation, such a claimant could not establish his claim against any particular employer, because he could not show that the mesothelioma would probably not have occurred "<u>but for</u>" the breach of duty by a <u>particular</u> employer.

Fairchild v Glenhaven Funeral Services Ltd[137]

4.17   The issue of causation, in cases of mesothelioma, was considered by the House of Lords in *Fairchild*. In a decision whereby their Lordships accepted that they were creating an exception to the usual "but for" test of causation, they held that policy reasons dictated that such a claimant could establish causation in the following circumstances:

---

[137]   [2002] UKHL 22

- He was employed by each defendant;
- Each defendant owed a duty to take reasonable care to prevent the claimant inhaling asbestos dust;
- Each defendant was in breach of that duty;
- The claimant suffered mesothelioma;
- Any cause of the claimant's mesothelioma other than inhalation of asbestos dust can be effectively discounted; and
- The claimant cannot prove on the balance of probabilities that the cause of mesothelioma was inhaling asbestos dust while working for one or other employer.

In such circumstances, the claimant is entitled to recover damages against <u>each defendant</u>.

4.18   The burden of proving breach of duty remains with the claimant as was pointed out by the Court of Appeal in *Brett v Reading University*[138]. The deceased had worked in a number of employments where he might have encountered asbestos, including his time as a clerk of work at the university. Reading University was the only defendant. The Court of Appeal considered that there were two questions to answer following *Fairchild as* follows:

- Did the defendant expose the deceased to asbestos?
- Was the defendant legally at fault?

4.19   The Court of Appeal decision turned on the second question. Sedley LJ put the matter as follows:

In other words did the university fail to take the necessary precautions to ensure that he did not inhale asbestos fibres? I put the question in this way, rather than asking whether the university took the necessary precautions, because on

---

[138]   [2007] EWCA Civ 88

principle it is for the claimant to establish the elements of his case, and one such element in a personal injury action is that the injury was caused by a breach of duty on the defendant's part.

It was not a defence to prove that the work was carried out by reputable contractors. Nevertheless, there was evidence that the contractors had been aware of the need to take precautions. The absence of documentary evidence showing that the precautions had actually been taken was not enough to impose liability on the defendants. Although there was sufficient evidence to enable the court to infer that the deceased had come into contact with asbestos in the course of his work at the university, the fact that he eventually developed mesothelioma did not enable the court to infer that the university had failed to take necessary steps to protect the claimant. Referring to *Fairchild* the Court of Appeal pointed out that although the deceased had worked in a number of jobs where he could have come into contact with asbestos, if there had been adequate evidence of breach of duty on the part of the university, his dependants would have succeeded in their action, notwithstanding the possible responsibility of other employers. However, in the absence of such evidence, the action against the university had to fail. An example of a case dealing with the first question posed in para 4.18 is *Willmore v Knowsley MBC*[139]. The claimant alleged that about 35 years previously she had attended a school at which she had been exposed to asbestos by:

- The removal of asbestos tiles from a ceiling and the stacking of those tiles in a corridor.
- The storage of broken asbestos tiles in the girls' toilets.

The Court of Appeal confirmed that a claimant must show that it was the "risk of harm" which the defendant created or

---

[139] [2009] EWCA Civ 1211

increased, and not simply the "risk of exposure" to asbestos fibres. In the case of asbestos Sedley LJ explained:

It has to be remembered that where asbestos is involved, a risk of exposure is a risk of harm. So long as there was evidence capable of justifying his findings, the conclusion that avoidable exposure in the school had made a material contribution to the risk and therefore to the eventual materialization of the claimant's illness was an entirely reasonable one.

In this case the Court of Appeal considered that there was enough evidence to allow the judge to conclude that there had been avoidable exposure to asbestos in the manner alleged.

Apportionment of damages

4.20   The question which came before the House of Lords for consideration in *Barker v Corus (UK) Ltd*[140] was whether each employer to whom the *Fairchild* exception applied, would be jointly and severally liable and therefore liable for the whole damage. Alternatively, would each employer only be liable for that part of the damage which he had caused, probably to be assessed on a time-line basis? This point had not been considered by the House of Lords in *Fairchild*.

4.21   The House of Lords considered that fairness meant that each employer to whom the *Fairchild* exception applied should only be liable to the extent that he had contributed. It was important to note that *Fairchild* had not decided that each defendant had <u>materially contributed to the injury</u>. Instead, *Fairchild had* decided that such employers should be liable on the basis that they had <u>created the risk of injury</u> and that "the creation of a material risk of mesothelioma was sufficient for liability". On the question of fairness, the

---

[140] [2006] UKHL 20

House of Lords considered that, on the one hand, the result of *Fairchild* meant that an employer could be held liable even though he had not caused the claimant's mesothelioma. This was because policy reasons dictated that where an employer was under a duty to take reasonable care to avoid his employees inhaling asbestos dust then it was appropriate that such employers should be liable to compensate the claimant. On the other hand, fairness indicated that in such circumstances, an employer should only be liable for his contribution to the probability that he caused the mesothelioma.

4.22   Within weeks of the House of Lords' decision in *Barker,* the government accepted criticism of the decision from trade unions and others, who pointed out that the decision could leave employees under-compensated if one or more of his previous employers were either no longer financially viable or uninsured. In the circumstances, by Section 3 of the Compensation Act, which came into force in July 2006, the effect of the decision in *Barker* was reversed so that employers to whom the *Fairchild* exception applies are jointly and severally liable for a claimant's damages and each employer is therefore liable to pay the whole amount of the claimant's damages. The question of apportionment is a matter to be dealt with between defendants, but does not concern the claimant.

4.23   Proof of causation following the decision in *Fairchild* and Section 3 of the Compensation Act 2006 was considered by the Court of Appeal in *Sienkewicz v Greif*[141], a claim brought on behalf of the estate of the deceased. The judge had found that the deceased had been tortiously exposed to asbestos by the defendant and that she had probably not been exposed to asbestos during any other employment. He also found, however, that the deceased had been exposed to low level of asbestos in the general atmosphere. The judge accepted that

---

[141]   [2009] EWCA Civ 1159

the claimant had to show that occupational exposure had at least doubled the risk of mesothelioma due to environmental exposure. The Court of Appeal had decided, in *Novartis Grimsby Limited v Cookson*[142], a case of bladder cancer, there had been evidence to the effect that the tortious exposure had more than doubled the risk arising from smoking and that that was sufficient for the claim to succeed. On behalf of the defendant in *Sienkewicz,* it was submitted that where it is, or should be, possible for the claimant to demonstrate that the tortious exposure has more than doubled the risk arising from any other exposure, he should be put to proof that such doubling of the risk had occurred. The *Fairchild* exception only applied where it was impossible for a claimant to demonstrate this.

4.24   The Court of Appeal noted, however, that the common law, on its own, no longer governs claims for damages in mesothelioma cases and referred to Section 3 of the Compensation Act 2006, which deals with mesothelioma and provides:

(1)   *This section applies where:*

(a) *A person ... has negligently ... caused or permitted another person ... to be exposed to asbestos,*

(b) *The victim has contracted mesothelioma as a result of exposure to asbestos,*

(c) *It is not possible to determine with certainty whether it was the exposure mentioned in paragraph (a) or another exposure which caused the victim to become ill, and*

(d) *The responsible person is liable in tort, by virtue of the exposure mentioned in paragraph (a) in connection with damage caused to the victim by the disease (whether by reason of having*

---

[142]   [2007] EWCA Civ 1261

materially increased a risk or for any other reason).

It was submitted on behalf of the defendant that the condition in paragraph 3(1)(d) was not satisfied and that it was plain that the claimant had to establish liability in tort at common law. The Court of Appeal disagreed. Smith LJ considered that Parliament had clearly provided that in all mesothelioma cases, a claimant can take advantage of Section 3 of the Compensation Act 2006;

provided that he or she can satisfy the four conditions in Section 3(1) and the fourth condition can, in my judgment, be satisfied by proof of causation by reference to a material increase in risk.

In the circumstances, the Court of Appeal held that in a mesothelioma case, it is not open to a defendant to put the claimant to proof of causation by reference to a two-fold increase in risk. In this case the tortious exposure had "materially increased the risk" and in such circumstances the claimant's case succeeded.

Limitation

4.25   In an action for personal injury alleging negligence, the ordinary limitation period within which an action is to be brought is three years from the occurrence of the cause of action, namely when the injury occurred. The case of *Cartledge v Jopling*[143] exposed an injustice arising out of the fact that the onset of asbestosis or mesothelioma will occur long after exposure to asbestos. The effect of S.11 of the Limitation Act 1980 is to extend the three year period so that it runs from the date on which the cause of action occurred or the date of knowledge (if later) of the person injured. Although the operation of the Limitation Act has given rise

---

[143]   [1963] AC 758

to problems in certain types of case [144] as Holland J said in *A B and others v Nugent Care Society,* in cases concerned with exposure to asbestos, "it is the court's experience that in such cases, limitation is rarely raised and certainly not to any effect".

Industrial Deafness

4.26   In 1963 a government appointed committee produced a report entitled "Noise". It contained a chapter on occupational exposure to high levels of noise, but concluded that the state of knowledge was not adequate to give a firm enough basis for legislation.

- The Department of Employment published a code of practice in 1972, which said that unless efficient hearing protectors were worn, employees should not be exposed to a level of noise over an 8-hour day exceeding 90dB(A).
- In 1990 the Noise at Work Regulations, 1989 came into effect. These were introduced to put into effect the Noise at Work Directive, 12 May 1986. The Regulations established two action levels:
- The first action level, 85dB(A)lepd, at which there should be a noise assessment. Adequate information, instruction and training was to be given to employees where noise exposure was likely to be at or exceed this level.
- The second action level, 90dB(A)lepd, at and over which level employees should not be exposed.

The 1989 Regulations also established a general duty on employers to reduce the risk of damage from exposure to noise to the lowest level reasonably practicable. This general

---

[144]   For example, education negligence - *Adams v Bracknell Forest BC* [2005] 1 AC 76 and "sexual abuse" cases eg. *A B and others v The Nugent Care Society 23* November 2006

duty even applied where noise exposure was below 85dB(A)lepd.

4.27   The noise at work regulations 1989 were matched in October 2000 by Railway Group Standard GM/RT 2160, published by the Safety and Standards Directorate of Railtrack Plc. These provided that train crew inside a railway vehicle should not be subjected to noise levels exceeding 84dB(A)lepd.

4.28   More recently, the Control of Noise at Work Regulations 2005 have followed the Noise at Work Directive, 6 February 2003. These Regulations say:

- Employees should not be exposed to noise levels above 87dB(A)lepd;
- Steps should be taken to reduce exposure, as far as practicable, where the noise level is likely to be above 85dB(A)lepd, and hearing protection must be provided;
- Where exposure is likely to be over 80dB(A)lepd, hearing protectors must be provided on request and there should be suitable instruction and training for employees.

4.29   In *Thompson v Smiths Ship Repairers (North Shields) Ltd*[145] the court held that after 1963, employers could not expect to defend a claim by relying on ignorance of the effects of noise and the means to provide protection for employees. The case did not address the question of noise levels as the noise exposure exceeded 90dB(A)lepd.

4.30   The Court of Appeal did consider exposure to noise levels below 90dB(A)lepd in *Harris v BRB (Residuary) Ltd*[146]. The claimant was an engine driver from 1970s until 1999. The level of noise to which he was exposed was over

---

[145]   [1984] 1 QB 405
[146]   [2005] EWCA Civ 900, [2005] ICR 1680

85dB(A)lepd, but lower than 90dB(A)lepd. British Rail had been warned by its medical officer, in 1973, that if drivers were exposed to noise at a level of 85dB(A)lepd for a period of 30 or 35 years, then it could be expected that between 6-8% of drivers would suffer hearing loss.

4.31   The Court of Appeal considered that this warning gave rise to a *"real, as opposed to minimal, risk of damage."* Once this was accepted, it must follow that, on the particular facts of a particular case, exposure of an employee to a level of sound at or over 85d8(A)Iepd could give rise to a duty of care. The technical documentation pointed to a conclusion that, at least until the 1989 Regulations came into force, an employer would not normally be expected to be liable to an employee who was exposed to a level of sound lower than 90dB(A)lepd, but this evidence could not go so far as to negate, in all circumstances, liability to employees whose health was impaired as a result of exposure to sound below that level. British Rail had been told of the risk in 1973 and accordingly the judge had been entitled to decide that they had been in breach of their duty to the claimant even though the noise levels had not exceeded 90dB(A)lepd.

4.32   The Court of Appeal gave further consideration to claims for noise induced hearing loss in *Baker v Quantum Clothing Group and others*[147], a case concerned with noise levels in the knitting industry, which were generally around 85dB(A)lepd. The judge had held that there had been no breach of the duty to provide a "safe place of work" under Section 29 of the Factories Act 1961 and that the general standard of safety was what should reasonably have been adopted by employers at the relevant time. Until at least 1987, when the 1986 Noise at Work Directive became generally known, the judge considered that it would be setting too high a standard to decide that employers were in

---

[147]   [2009] EWCA Civ 499, [2009] PIQR P19

breach of their duty of care to employees if complying with the 1972 guidelines.

4.33   The Court of Appeal disagreed and held that the duty under Section 29 of the Factories Act 1961 is absolute, subject to a defence of "reasonable practicability". There is no requirement on a claimant to show that an injury was reasonably foreseeable. The Department of Employment Code of Practice 1972 had said that prolonged exposure to noise levels of 85dB(A)lepd was harmful to some people. Employers with noisy processes should have known of the Code of Practice, and by mid 1973 should have been considering the problem of noise. Such employers would have known that, in terms of Section 29 of the Factories Act 1961, a place of work was "unsafe" for an undefined section of the workforce. At this point they were under a statutory duty to take "reasonably practicable" steps to eliminate the risk of noise induced hearing loss. The Court of Appeal accepted that it would not have been easy for employers to quantify the risk until publication of British Standard BS5330 in July 1976. Average sized employers in the knitting industry would have been able to make an informed assessment of the risk arising from noise levels below 90dB(A)lepd by early 1977. The provision of ear protectors was neither difficult nor expensive and the defendants should have provided them by January 1978. Since January 1978, therefore, an employer will have been in breach of Section 29 of the Factories Act 1961 where an employee has been exposed to noise levels in excess of 85dB(A)lepd if hearing protection has not been provided.

4.34   *Baker* was one of a number of claimants whose cases were considered at first instance. On the facts of the cases, none of the other claimants were able to establish that they were suffering from noise induced hearing loss. At trial, the judge considered how he would have apportioned damages between different periods of causative employment, had he found in favour of the claimants. He said that in the absence of particular evidence, damages would probably be apportioned on a time-line basis, however, he did not rule out the possibility that the evidence in some cases might point to a more severe hearing loss during earlier years of employment.

Injury Caused by Vibration

4.35   As in the case of noise levels, guidance has been provided, over the years, on the effects of vibration on hand and arm, and on the body as a whole. The use of vibrating tools can give rise to vibration induced white finger ("VWF") and hand-arm vibration syndrome ("HAVS"). Whole body vibration can cause injury such as back injury.

4.36   In 1975, the British Standards Institution ("BSI") published DD43, a "guide to the evaluation of exposure of the human hand-arm system to vibration". In 1987, the BSI issued BS6842, "measurement and evaluation of human exposure to vibration transmitted to the hand". Again, in 1987, the BSI published BS6841, "measurement and evaluation of human exposure to whole body mechanical vibration and repeated shock". The aim was to provide uniform methods of measuring vibration. Both documents indicated levels of vibration over a daily eight-hour period at which injury could be expected in a percentage of the workforce exposed for a period of years.

4.37   The Health and Safety Executive issued a publication, "hand-arm vibration" in 1994. This recommended programmes of preventive measures and health surveillance where workers' exposure to vibration regularly exceeded the "action level" (2.8 M/S2), and then said:

A preventive program should control the risk of injury if introduced where there is prolonged use of tools likely to be hazardous, or where it is known that vibration exposure will exceed the "action level".

4.38   Railway Group Standard GM/RT2160, published by the
        Safety and Standards Directorate of Railtrack Plc in October
        2000, provided a vibration limit above which a train crew
        should not be subjected to during a working day. More
        recently, the Control of Vibration at Work Regulations 2005
        provides a limit for the amount of vibration an employee
        may be exposed to on any single day. An employer must
        assess the amount of vibration risk to employees and if the
        employees are likely to be exposed above the relevant level,
        the employer must take steps to eliminate or reduce the daily
        exposure to vibration so far as is reasonably practicable.

4.39   In *Billington and another v British Rail Engineering Ltd*[148]
        the claim concerned hand-arm vibration syndrome. The
        claimants had not been exposed to vibration exceeding the
        "action level" mentioned in the 1994 HSE publication.
        Nevertheless, Field J found in favour of the claimants. He
        relied on the HSE publication and, in particular, he held that
        a preventive programme should have been introduced, as
        there had been a "prolonged use of tools likely to be
        hazardous". He said:

> *In my view, the work done by the claimant and the other*
> *regular users of vibrating tools was 'regular, prolonged use,*
> *likely to be hazardous.' However, the defendants neither*
> *measured the exposure levels of the claimants and the other*
> *regular users of vibrating tools nor treated such use of*
> *vibrating tools as regular prolonged use likely to be*
> *hazardous. The defendants accordingly did not act in*
> *compliance with the 1994 HSE document and therefore*
> *cannot in my opinion shelter behind that guidance.*

4.40   The case of *Billington* was distinguished in *Clough v*
        Northwestern Trains Co Ltd[149], a case involving whole body
        vibration. The court concluded that the claimant's exposure

---

[148]   [2002] EWHC 105
[149]   (Unreported) 16 September 2005

to vibration was below the level at which BS6841 suggested that employers should take caution. In the circumstances, the claim failed. The difference between this case and that of *Billington* was that while in the latter case there was evidence of prolonged use of tools likely to be hazardous, which should have caused the employer to undertake a preventive programme of surveillance, there was not the same evidence in *Clough* and the judge considered that if a survey had been carried out, it would not have led the employers to conclude that the claimant's back injury was due to whole body vibration caused by the defendant's trains.

4.41   In both *Billington* and *Clough* reference was made to *Stokes v Guest* and *Keen and Nettlefold*[150], where Swanwick J said:

The overall test is still the conduct of the reasonable and prudent employer, taking positive thought for the safety of his workers in the light of what he knows or ought to know.

The employer had such knowledge in *Billington*, but not in the case of *Clough*.

4.42   In *Allison v London Underground Limited*[151] the claimant was an underground train driver who developed Tenosynovitis by her constant holding of the brake controller. The case concerned the issue of training under the Provision and Use of Work Equipment Regulations 1988. Although under Regulation 9, the duty to provide training is mandatory, the Court of Appeal did not consider that this introduced no-fault liability because to do so would require clear wording. The "adequacy of the training was to be judged in the light of what the employer knew or ought to have known, about the risks arising from his business, taking professional advice where necessary. In this case, the defendants should have obtained advice from a suitable

---

[150]   [1968] I WLR 1776
[151]   [2008] EWCA Civ 71

expert before putting the brake controller into service. Had this happened, the advice would have identified the need for drivers to be trained in the use of the brake controller.

Limitation in Noise Induced Hearing Loss and Vibration Claims

4.43   In dealing with limitation in cases of noise induced hearing loss and hand-arm vibration syndrome ("HAVS"), courts have applied the tests for actual and constructive knowledge under Section 14 of the Limitation Act 1980 more liberally than in the case of asbestos related claims.

4.44   A claimant's date of knowledge for limitation purposes is defined in Section 14(1)(a) as the date when he first had knowledge that the injury in question was "significant", which is defined in Section 14(2). The definition of a "significant" injury was considered by the Court of Appeal in *McCoubrey v Ministry of Defence*[152], a claim for traumatic hearing loss suffered by a soldier. The court confirmed that when considering whether an injury was "significant" the test is an objective test, namely whether the injury itself was significant and not whether the injury had a significant impact on the claimant.

4.45   Similarly, the test for constructive knowledge under Section 14(3) of the Limitation Act 1980 is an objective test. In *Adams v Bracknell Forest Borough Council* [153], a case concerned with Education Negligence, Lord Hoffman said:

> *In my opinion, Section 14(3) requires one to assume that a person who is aware that he has suffered a personal injury, serious enough to be something about which he would go and see a solicitor if he knew he had a claim, will be sufficiently curious about the causes of the injury to seek whatever expert advice is appropriate.*

---

[152]   [2007] EWCA Civ 17
[153]   [2004] UKHL 29

4.46   In cases involving noise induced hearing loss and hand-arm vibration syndrome, courts have been more willing to find that claimants had the requisite knowledge for the purpose of Section 14 of the Limitation Act 1980. As a result, cases are more likely to be decided under Section 33 of the Limitation Act under which the court has an unfettered discretion to disallow the limitation period and allow a claim to continue. Although in *KR v Bryn Alyn Community (Holdings) Limited*[154] the exercise of the court's discretion under Section 33 of the Limitation Act 1980 was described as an "exceptional indulgence", it seems clear that courts will be prepared to allow claims to proceed. In *Cain v Francis*[155] Smith LJ considered that the test was whether it was "fair and just to allow the action to proceed". The court must balance the prejudice suffered by the claimant, if the claim is held to be statute barred against the prejudice suffered by the defendant in defending the claim, if it is allowed to proceed.

Work-related Upper Limb Disorder

4.47   In work of a repetitive nature, there is a duty to warn employees of the risk of work-related upper limb disorder. In *Peppall v Thorn Consumers Electronics Limited*[156], Woolf LJ held that there is a duty on an employer to give a warning of the risk of work-related upper limb disorder before the employment begins. An employee can therefore either decide not to do the work, or know that an early manifestation of the problem in question should be reported to the employer to enable preventive steps to be taken. The warning must therefore include an explanation as to why it must be reported.

4.48   The House of Lords considered work-related upper limb

---

[154]   [2003] QB 1441
[155]   [2008] WLR (D) 43
[156]   (Unreported) 20 December 1985

disorder in *Pickford v Imperial Chemical Industries*[157]. The claimant was a secretary who alleged that she had developed PDA4, a recognised industrial disease (cramp of the hand), because of her typing load. The House of Lords heard that PDA4 might have an organic cause or a psychogenic (imagined) cause, or a combination of the two, and held that the burden of proof was on the claimant to satisfy the court that her cramp had an organic cause. A similar issue was considered by the Court of Appeal in *Alexander and Others v Midland Bank plc*[158]. The Court of Appeal confirmed that the claimant had to establish a causal link between any breach of duty and the injury. On the facts of the case, the court considered that the defendant had been well aware of the risk of work-related upper limb disorder and had failed to organise the claimant's work so as to give her adequate breaks.

4.49 Cases involving work related upper limb disorder will now involve consideration of Regulations such as the Management of Health and Safety at Work Regulations 1999 and the Health and Safety (Display Screen Equipment) Regulations 1992. In *Fifield v Denton Hall Legal Services and Others*[159], the claimant alleged that she suffered work-related upper limb disorder as a result of an increase in her keyboard workload. The Court of Appeal accepted that there had been breaches of the 1992 Regulations because the risk assessment had been inadequate and there was no evidence that the claimant had received any training in the use of her workstation.

[157] [1998] 3 All ER 462 [1998] 1 WLR 1189
[158] [2000] ICR 464
[159] [2006] EWCA Civ 169

FIVE

CLAIMS ALLOCATION AND HANDLING AGREEMENT (CAHA)

Introduction

5.1   Following the privatisation of British Rail in 1994, the industry was broken up into separate companies and other organisations. To enable a member of the travelling public to confidently bring a claim against a rail industry party, the Government made it a condition of obtaining an operating licence for any company operating railway assets, to adopt approved arrangements for handling claims. It was also envisaged that by adopting such an arrangement for handling claims, it would avoid a situation where one rail industry party, faced with a claim by a member of the travelling public, would seek to avoid liability by blaming one or more other rail industry parties. The simplest way of satisfying this licence condition has been for a rail industry party to become a signatory to CAHA.

5.2   The first Agreement was signed on 1 April 1994. The most recent consolidated version of the Agreement is dated 1 December 2009. There are, in March 2010, 62 authorised CAHA parties who are all signatories to the agreement. They are listed in Schedule 6 of the Agreement.

It should be noted that parties can be added or withdrawn from CAHA (clause 20). Furthermore, CAHA can be incorporated into contracts with independent contractors who are not already signatories to the Agreement (clause 15).

Allocation of third party liabilities

5.3   CAHA applies to a claim brought against any CAHA party arising in connection with the operation of railway assets or on land owned or controlled by a CAHA party. CAHA does not apply to claims where the cause of action occurred prior to 1 April 1994. The practical implication of this exemption is that many occupational disease claims (those where there was negligent exposure prior to 1 April 1994) are not covered by CAHA (see clause 2.1).

The Registrar and the Rail Industry Dispute Resolution Committee

5.4   The CAHA Registrar is the custodian of the agreement and is responsible for matters of administration and for holding the signed original. The Registrar will, amongst other things, identify Lead Parties and Potentially Liable Parties, allocate claims and is the first "port of call" in respect of any disputes between CAHA parties. The Registrar is a non-profit making position funded by an annual levy on CAHA parties. The Registrar's obligations are set out in Schedule 2 of CAHA. The Rail Industry Dispute Resolution (RIDR) Committee seeks to resolve disputes in an informal and inexpensive manner between rail industry parties. The RIDR Committee has defined rules governing its operation, which can be found at http://www.ridr.co.uk/.

Threshold

5.5   CAHA sets out the means of allocating claims depending on their value. It distinguishes claims on whether the final liability is likely to be less than or equal to the Threshold, or if there is insufficient information to determine whether or not the final liability is likely to be less than or equal to the threshold.

5.6   Final liability is the amount required to be paid to a claimant by a CAHA party under a judgment, decree or settlement in respect of a claim. In each case interest is included but costs are not included. The current Threshold is £7,500.

Employers' liability claims equal to or below the Threshold

5.7   Claims where the final liability is, or is likely to be less than £7,500 will be allocated to the employer. That is to say, liability for such a claim brought by an employee or former employee of a CAHA party who suffered loss or damage in the course of his or her employment with the CAHA party shall be borne by the CAHA party who employs or employed the claimant at the relevant time (clause 2.2).

5.8   It is open to the CAHA parties involved in the claim to agree to depart from the usual operation of clause 2.2. It is also open to the CAHA party who is the employer to invite the Registrar to reallocate liability. However, the starting point is that the employer must handle the claim.

Public liability claims equal to or below the Threshold

5.9   Public liability claims equal to or below the £7,500 Threshold are allocated in accordance with Schedule 1 of CAHA. The Schedule describes 32 different types of claims' scenarios and the corresponding responsible CAHA party. By way of illustration, where a claim involves damage to property or personal injury on stations, the CAHA party in legal occupation of that part of the station on which the damage or injury occurred will be the responsible party, but where damage to property or personal injury occurs when boarding or alighting a train the CAHA party under whose licence, or European licence, the train is operated will be the responsible party. For damage to property or personal injury which occurs on a train, however caused but with the example of vandalism, the responsible party is again the CAHA party under whose licence, or European licence, the train is operated. Where damage to property or personal injury occurs at a level crossing, the infrastructure manager or CAHA party in legal occupation of the level crossing is the responsible party.

Claims above the Threshold

5.10   If the amount of final liability exceeds the Threshold, liability shall be borne by the CAHA party or parties who would be liable for the loss at law (clause 2.3). CAHA does not apply to allocate such claims.

Handling of Claims below the Threshold

5.11   Any CAHA party (or the Registrar) who receives a claim believed to be below the Threshold (or equal to the Threshold) must send it promptly to the CAHA party apparently bearing liability in accordance with the Agreement. That is to say, an employer in an employers' liability claim or the relevant industry party under Schedule 1 of CAHA in respect of a public liability claim.

5.12   If the CAHA party who has been forwarded the claim disputes its responsibility under Schedule 1, it must send the claim to the Registrar, unless it has been received from the Registrar, in which case that CAHA party must deal with the claim and, if appropriate, make arrangements for paying the claim. It is open to that CAHA party to refer any disputed liability to the Railway Industry Dispute Resolution (RIDR) Committee. If the RIDR Committee determines that liability should rest with another CAHA party, that other CAHA party must reimburse any amounts paid plus interest (see clauses 8 and 9.15 to 9.18).

Handling of Claims above the Threshold

5.13   Clause 9 of CAHA deals with the management of claims over the Threshold. If any CAHA party becomes aware of a claim, or an event that gives rise to a claim, that CAHA party shall notify the Registrar and the Registrar shall serve a notice under clause 9.1 to all Potentially Liable Parties. In claims above the Threshold involving more than one CAHA party, it is therefore likely that there will be a Lead Party and one or more Potentially Liable Parties.

5.14   The Lead Party must give due consideration to the interests of all Potentially Liable Parties. In practice, this will involve updating all Potentially Liable Parties with regards to the progress of the claim/litigation. It follows that it is advisable to obtain authority from all Potentially Liable Parties prior to settlement of a claim. The Lead Party will manage the claim and, except in the case of a 'major incident', shall fund any interim payments, reasonable expenses (to include legal expenses) on behalf of the Potentially Liable Parties. Following agreement or termination of the claim, the Lead Party can invoice the relevant Potential Liable Parties accordingly.

5.15   In the event of a dispute with regard to liability for a claim between the Lead Party and one or more Potentially Liable Parties, it is not open for the Lead Party to ask a Court (in the event that the matter proceeds to a Court hearing) to allocate liability between it and the other Potentially Liable Parties. It is not open for a CAHA party to bring Court proceedings (under Part 20 of the Civil Procedural Rules or by any other means) against another CAHA party. Any issues as to apportionment of liability must be dealt with by agreement or by reference to the RIDR Committee or by reference to the RIDR Committee, if appropriate. As early as possible in the life of a claim the Lead Parties should attempt to agree with the Potentially Liable Parties how liability to the claimant should be split between them. If agreement is not possible, the Lead Party will advise the Registrar, who, if unable to facilitate an agreement will refer this dispute to the RIDR Committee.

5.16   It is also worthy of note that there is a code of practice for use by those who are handling claims on behalf of a CAHA party. The code applies to claims made on or after 1 April 1998. Part B of the code sets out principles governing the conduct of the claim. These are: the claim should be handled efficiently and responsibly; claims should be handled courteously without taking advantage of lack of knowledge or resource of the claimant; and once compensation is agreed, the amount to be fair and reasonable and paid without delay.

Independent Contractors

5.17   The CAHA party contracting with an independent contractor must, if reasonably practical, bind the contractor to CAHA. In respect of the discharge of that contract, the contractor will effectively become a CAHA party.

Property damage

5.18   Subject to the terms of any specific contract between them, a CAHA party may recover its losses in respect of damage to property from another CAHA party resulting from a single event or circumstances arising from the operation of railway assets occurring after 1 May 2004, for which one or more CAHA party would be liable at law. The loss must exceed £10,000 and is subject to a cap of £5,000,000 (clause 16). It should be noted that CAHA parties are prohibited from recovering consequential losses (for example loss of fair revenue, or goodwill) from any other CAHA party (clause 17).

Provision of information

5.19   A CAHA party, or a party handling a claim on behalf of a CAHA party, may request any relevant document from another CAHA party, subject to legal privilege, to be provided to assist in the investigation and consideration of a claim. Furthermore, any individual who the CAHA party or Registrar considers to be able to provide relevant information should be made available to the CAHA party handling the claim so that the individual can be interviewed.

The Passenger Rights Regulation

5.20   On 3 December 2009 a new EU Regulation came into force (Regulation No 1371/2007) relating to passengers' rights and obligations. The EU Regulation had direct force in the UK without the need for national legislation to implement it. The Regulation has resulted in some amendments to CAHA, which were reflected in the 1 December 2009 consolidated version. However, the Regulations will have little application to train operating companies in the UK. This is because the UK Government passed the Rail Passengers' Rights and Obligations (Exemption) Regulations 2009 which took effect on 4 December 2009 and has the effect that the Passenger Rights Regulation are not applicable to domestic rail passenger services in the UK. It is still applicable to international services in the UK (i.e. Eurostar at present).

5.21   The advanced payment provision (Article 13 of the Regulation) states: "a passenger who is injured is entitled to an advance payment from the Railway undertaking". This point is no longer of concern to domestic operators in the UK given the exemption Regulation, but could be applicable as a matter of law to any CAHA party offering international services.

SIX

HEALTH AND SAFETY REGULATION AND ENFORCEMENT IN THE RAIL SECTOR

Introduction

6.1　This chapter aims to provide an overview and guide to dealing with workplace health and safety in the rail sector from a criminal enforcement perspective. The overview provided should serve to equip claims' managers and employers with the necessary tools to defend their position in the event of a serious accident or fatality. From high profile accidents to the movement of vehicles on site, Health and Safety law governs a huge breadth of issues within the railway industry. This section details the correct approaches to managing health and safety, the chief offences under the principal legislation, and best practice guidance on managing and responding to a post-incident investigation.

Regulatory Bodies and The Rail Sector

6.2　The rail sector is subject to its own regulatory framework, which has developed since the 1993 privatisation of British Rail.

6.3　The Office of Rail Regulation ("ORR") replaced the position of Rail Regulator on 5 July 2004 which was established following privatisation on 5 November 1993. It has the dual function of providing economic and health and safety regulation to the rail sector. The economic function is carried out by determining the level of funding required by Network Rail based on reviews of the costs and requirements of the work to be conducted.

6.4   The health and safety role has been transferred from the Health and Safety Executive ("HSE") to the ORR and as such its activities in the rail context are identical to those of the HSE in other fields under the Health and Safety at Work etc Act 1974 ("HASWA"). The ORR therefore is concerned with safeguarding the safety of employees; passengers and third parties. The ambit of the ORR's powers extends to the London Underground and trams as well as conventional rail.

6.5   For the purposes of health and safety enforcement any activity carried out in connection with a railway, tramway or similar guided transport system is within the remit of the ORR under the Health and Safety (Enforcing Authority for Railways and Other Guided Transport Systems) Regulations 2006[160]. The ORR publishes an enforcement policy and subscribes to the HSE's Enforcement Management Model to ensure consistency in decision making.

6.6   Her Majesty's Rail Inspectorate ("HMRI") implements the strategies of the ORR through checks and inspections, to assess risk management systems and monitor their effectiveness including particular scrutiny of high risk areas. HMRI also has conduct of the enforcement regime and investigation for suspected health and safety offences. HMRI performs a similar function to that carried out by HSE Inspectors and local authority Environmental Health Officers in other industry sectors. References to "inspectors" in this chapter can be considered to include HMRI.

6.7   The Railway Industry Advisory Committee ("RIAC") has a long history of providing advice on rail safety and produces guidance on health & safety and other issues and this function has been maintained under the present regime.

6.8   Impartial investigation for fact-finding purposes into rail accidents is conducted by the Rail Accident Investigation

---

[160]   SI 2006/557

Branch ("RAIB"). Their purpose is to ensure that the industry learns from accidents and to propose means of preventing recurrence. Following an investigation HMRI have responsibility for adopting and carrying out RAIB's recommendations.

6.9   The Rail Safety and Standards Board ("RSSB") is a forum for various stakeholders, which aims to assist and champion health and safety performance in the rail sector. It has a variety of functions including the management of Railway Group Standards; measuring safety and risk across the industry; leading research and development; producing the Strategic Safety Plan; and providing expertise and guidance to the industry.

6.10   In addition the EU has an increasing role in rail regulation and has produced several directives harmonising rail standards across Europe which have been implemented into UK health and safety law, as can be seen, for example, in the Railway Safety Directive[161] which introduced mandatory requirements for Safety Management Systems; certification for managers and the provision of training services.

The Key Provisions of Health and Safety Legislation:

6.11   The leading health and safety legislation is Health and Safety at Work Etc Act 1974 ("HASWA") which imposes the basic duties on employers to safeguard their employees' safety.

6.12   Supplementing HASWA are six regulations known as the "six pack", which are the Management of Health and Safety at Work Regulations 1999 (as amended) ("the Management Regulations"); the Workplace (Health Safety and Welfare) Regulations 1992 (as amended); the Provision and Use of Work Equipment Regulations 1998 (as amended) ("PUWER"); the Personal Protective Equipment Regulations

---

[161] 2004/49/EC as amended by Directive 2008/110/EC

1992 (as amended); the Manual Handling Operations Regulations 1992 (as amended) and the Health and Safety (Display Screen Equipment) Regulations 1992 (as amended). In addition, further regulations of general application include the Work at Height Regulations 2005 and the Control of Substances Hazardous to Health Regulations 2002 ("COSHH"). Some regulations are industry specific but many are of general application and create absolute duties which must be complied with whatever the practicalities or cost. Failure to comply will amount to an offence on the part of an employer company.

6.13   A detailed analysis of Health and Safety Regulation is outside the scope of this book, however, it is possible to give an introduction to the key concepts.

Duties Under HASWA

6.14   HASWA creates employer duties to do all that is reasonably practicable to ensure the health, safety and welfare of employees[162] and everyone else who is likely to be affected by a business[163]. This duty applies to any undertaking (meaning that it potentially applies to self employed persons as well as employers) and can extend to the safety of sub-contractors, suppliers, customers and the public at large.

6.15   The reasonably practicable qualification requires a balancing exercise between the likelihood and potential nature of the harm arising from a risk on one side and the costs and burdens of avoiding or mitigating the risk on the other. What is reasonably practicable will vary widely between duty holders and circumstances and will be a question of fact to be determined in each set of particular circumstances.

---

[162] Section 2 HASWA
[163] Section 3 HASWA

6.16   To succeed with a prosecution for a breach of HASWA the prosecution need only establish the existence of a risk after which the burden will fall to the employer to prove that all reasonably practicable steps were taken to prevent the risk (*R v Board of Trustees of the Science Museum*[164]). In the aftermath of a workplace accident the threshold for the prosecution to overcome is a relatively low one as the fact of an accident's occurrence will be strongly indicative of the existence of a risk.

6.17   For present purposes this is known as a "reverse burden", in which is it up to the defendant to rebut the assumption of a breach by demonstrating reasonable practicability. This differs from the normal criminal law in which it is for the prosecution to prove their case beyond reasonable doubt before the defence need make any submissions.

6.18   HASWA applies to all work activities and imposes duties on employers which include:

- S2(1)   ensuring so far as is reasonably practicable the health, safety and welfare of employees;
- S3(1)   so far as is reasonably practicable to avoid conducting their undertaking in such a way as to expose persons not in their employment to risk;
- S2(2)   ensuring that the plant, premises and machinery do not endanger operatives.

6.19   It also imposes duties on employees to:

- S7(a)   safeguard their own and one another's health;
- S7(b)   co-operate with their employer;
- S8   not intentionally or recklessly interfere with or misuse articles provided for health and safety.

---

[164] [1993] 3 All ER 853

6.20   It is an offence under section 33 to breach any of these duties subject to the section 40 qualification that no offence is committed where the accused proves that it did all that was reasonably practicable. This reverse burden was challenged in the case of *David Janway Davies v Health and Safety Executive*[165] in a challenge under the Human Rights Act 1998. The court held that it was necessary, proportionate and justified to protect the health and safety of workers and that *"the facts relied on in support of the defence should not be difficult to prove because they will be within the knowledge of the defendant. Whether the defendant should have done more will be judged objectively".*

Other General Duties

6.21   Duties to provide appropriate work equipment are imposed by various enactments including PUWER and the Personal Protective Equipment at Work Regulations 1992 (as amended). The former requires that the equipment provided be suitable and safe and the latter requires that appropriate protective clothing and equipment be provided.

6.22   There are also regulations concerning the way in which a workplace is established, equipped and run such as the Workplace (Health Safety and Welfare) Regulations 1992 (covering temperature, lighting, drinking water, toilets, first aid, etc.); the Health and Safety (First Aid) Regulations 1981; the Health and Safety (Display Screen Equipment) Regulations 1992 and COSHH.

6.23   The Health and Safety system in the UK relies largely on self reporting of accidents by employers in accordance with the Reporting of Injuries, Diseases and Dangerous Occurrences Regulations 1995 ("RIDDOR")[166] which require major injuries; deaths; dangerous occurrences;

---

[165]   [2002] EWCA Crim 2949
[166]   OSI 1995/3163

hospitalisations; occupational diseases; and accidents causing over 3 days of absence to be reported. Failure to report is, in itself, a criminal offence.

6.24   The rail sector also has specific obligations. The Railways Act 1993 brought the railways within HASWA. The Railways Act 2005 transferred responsibility for safety regulation to the ORR and the Railways (Safety Case) Regulations 2000[167] amended the safety case system. The latter Regulations have now been replaced by the Railways and Other Guided Systems (Safety) Regulations 2006[168] ("ROGS") which implemented various European directives relating to railway safety whilst the Railways (Access to Training Services) Regulations 2006[169] provided access to the relevant training services.

6.25   The chief requirement of the ROGS is to impose requirements that operators and managers maintain Safety Management Systems and hold an authorisation/safety certificate respectively confirming the ORR's approval.

Assessing Risk

6.26   Risk assessment is the cornerstone of health and safety. The Management Regulations impose a duty to risk assess; where there are five or more employees the employer must record this assessment. There are also obligations concerning implementing measures; provision of information and training and the appointment of competent persons.

6.27   In practice, only if it is grossly disproportionate to avoid or reduce the risk will the standard be satisfied by inaction. The case of *R v HTM Ltd*[170] confirmed that the possibility or

---

[167]   OSI 2000/2688
[168]   OSI 2006/1599
[169]   OSI 2006/598
[170]   [2006] EWCA Crim 1156

nature of a risk has to be foreseeable, the law therefore does not require reasonably practicable control measures to be taken in relation to unforeseeable or "everyday" risks of life but recognises that health and safety evolves over time as new risks become apparent[171]. Risk assessments must be reviewed and modified on a regular basis and not only as the nature of the business changes, but also in response to additional risks that may become apparent over time, for example as a result of accidents. This is endorsed by HSE guidance[172] in relation to the preparation of risk assessments.

6.28   The standard to be met is an objective one and will involve an examination of what was known or ought to have been known to be a risk both within that business and in the industry generally.

6.29   The required approach in managing risk is to avoid risk entirely and, where this is not possible, to mitigate it so as to reduce it to the lowest practicable level. Generally an employer's ignorance of a risk will not provide any defence provided that that risk was one which should have been foreseen. However where an employee is acting far outside of his normal work functions or where an employer, in spite of appropriate risk management systems, does not know or suspect the existence of a risk, then it may fall outside of the burdens posed by the reasonable practicability test. These concepts are discussed in more detail in *Employer's Undertaking and Foreseeability of Risk* (paras 6.64 - 6.72).

Health and Safety Corporate Liability

6.30   Companies are persons in law, and this means that they have a legal persona which is distinct from their shareholders and directors. Indeed there is a public interest in ensuring that the

---

[171] For further discussion of foreseeability see "*Employer's Undertaking and Foreseeability of Risk*" (paras 6.64 – 6.72).
[172] HSE Book *Reducing Risks Protecting People*

financial liabilities of a company are not payable by its members. It is well established in law that a company and its members are distinct and only in rare circumstances such as fraud will this "veil of incorporation" be pierced[173].

6.31   Obviously a company has no mind to which decisions can be attributed, meaning that companies cannot be liable for certain offences, such as theft, as it is impossible to demonstrate the necessary intent. Nevertheless certain offences, known as strict or absolute liability offences, which only require the performance of the requisite action, can be committed by a company.

6.32   Examples of strict liability offences include motoring offences such as speeding in which it does not matter whether there is an intention to exceed the speed limit, the mere act of doing so is sufficient to commit an offence. Thus strict liability requires no mental element, absolute liability on the other hand means that provided the relevant act is committed no defence is available. In most health and safety offences both definitions are satisfied and they are known as "qualified duty" offences. This refers to the fact that if a company is prosecuted for failing to comply with this duty, then once a risk is proven it is for the company to satisfy a Court that it has taken all reasonably practicable steps to ensure the health and safety of the various persons to whom it owes a duty. This is known as a reverse burden of proof but is often incorrectly referred to as a defence.

6.33   Where a company is an employer it owes duties to its employees under the various enactments. These duties are non delegable[174], meaning that even if an individual, such as a health and safety manager, is made responsible for ensuring the safety of employees, the company cannot attempt to point the finger of blame and thereby escape

---

[173] *A Salomon & Co v Salomon* [1897] AC 22, HL
[174] *R v British Steel* [1995] 1 W.L.R. 1356

liability. Whilst this person may be liable individually for separate offences (see below), primary liability will reside with the company.

6.34   In addition, corporate criminal liability is vicarious, meaning that a company can be liable for actions of its employees, even in some cases where these actions are not ones which the company authorised.

6.35   Recently the statutory offence of Corporate Manslaughter[175] replaced the common law offence which depended on finding a director who had sufficient authority and involvement to be shown as the "directing mind and will". If this individual was potentially liable for gross negligence manslaughter then liability could also be imputed to the company. In practice, for large businesses, this was extremely difficult to prove. A good example is the prosecution for the Hatfield derailment in which charges of corporate manslaughter were dismissed against both Balfour Beatty and Railtrack due to insufficient evidence of an individual director's responsibility, knowledge and neglect in relation to the incident itself. The new statutory offence aims to overcome these difficulties.[176]

Health and Safety Individual Liability

6.36   Health and Safety legislation also requires that workers assist in implementing its requirements.

6.37   Section 7 of HASWA creates a separate offence for employees at work and provides that it shall be the duty of every employee while at work to take reasonable care for health and safety of themselves and of other persons who may be affected by his acts or omissions at work and to co-operate with his employer in respect to any duty or

---

[175] See *Corporate Manslaughter and Corporate Homicide Act 2007*
[176] See *Corporate Manslaughter* (paras 6.131 – 6.136)

requirement imposed on the employer by the statutory provisions, so far as is necessary to enable that duty or requirement to be performed or complied with. The duty under this section will apply to every level of employee including directors and officers and is in addition to the general duties of an employer as set out above.

6.38   The second raft of individual offences are created by Section 37 of the Health and Safety at Work Act. It provides that where an offence under any of the relevant statutory provisions committed by a body corporate is proved to have been committed with the consent or connivance of, or to have been attributable to any neglect on the part of any director, manager, secretary or other similar officer of the body corporate or a person who was purporting to act in any such capacity, he as well as the body corporate shall be guilty of that offence, and should be liable to be proceeded against and punished accordingly.

6.39   Unlike section 37 breaches of section 7 are capable of being prosecuted without an admission of guilt by, or prosecution of, the employer. In practice such prosecutions are usually brought against lower level employees where their own actions may have brought about or contributed to the circumstances giving rise to breach.

6.40   It is established law that no director owes a duty to ensure that a company is complying with the law simply as a result of holding the office of director. Furthermore, there are currently no statutory duties placed upon directors of companies in relation to health and safety, nor does a director of a company owe any duty, statutory or otherwise, to employees or others in respect of the company's compliance with any health and safety duties it owes simply by holding the office of director. This may however change in the future.

6.41 Liability under Section 37 however, requires proof of any one (or more) of the three different heads, namely consent, connivance and neglect. Unlike the position generally under, for example Section 2 of HASWA, where it is for a company to satisfy a court that it has taken all reasonably practicable steps to ensure the health and safety of the people to whom it owes a duty, for prosecutions under Section 37 it is for the Crown to prove their case against the individual.

6.42 Liability under section 37 requires that an offence has been proven against the company, thus such a prosecution cannot stand on its own but requires proof of, or an admission of, an offence's commission by the employer. Thus, for instance, an acceptance of a Simple Caution (see *Cautions* below) by an employer could potentially lay its directors open to charges under section 37.

Consent

6.43 For consent, a director must be proven to have known the material facts which constituted any offence by the company and to have agreed to the conduct of its business on the basis of those facts.

Connivance

6.44 For connivance, proof is required of the directors' "wilful blindness" (an intentional shutting of the eyes). It has been established that a director is conniving if he:

> *is well aware of what is going on but his agreement is tacit, not actively encouraging what happens but letting it continue and saying nothing about it*[177].

Neglect

6.45 The third heading of liability under Section 37 is potentially

---

[177] *Huckerby v Elliott* [1970] 1 All ER 189

the most onerous. The recent case of *R v P*[178] extended the law significantly in this area. The HSE alleged that the managing director had ultimate responsibility for ensuring the company's compliance with safe systems of work. The Court of Appeal held that a director was guilty of an offence under Section 37 if he either knew of the relevant facts or if he ought to have "been put on enquiry as to whether or not the appropriate safety procedures were in place". This will depend on the circumstances and facts of each case.

6.46   Lord Hope's remarks *in R v Chargot Ltd*[179] also give a useful guide:

> *It will be a relatively short step for the inference to be drawn that there was connivance or neglect on his part if the circumstances under which the risk arose were under the direction or control of the officer. The more remote his area of responsibility is from those circumstances, the harder it will be to draw that inference.*

Manslaughter

6.47   The Corporate Manslaughter and Corporate Homicide Act 2007 introduced an offence of Corporate Manslaughter which replaced the pre-existing liability of corporations under the common law for manslaughter and the new offence is incapable of individual application under section 18. (For further discussion of the offence of Corporate Manslaughter see *Corporate Manslaughter paras 6.131 - 6.136*). This was in response to the failed prosecutions following the Hatfield rail crash[180] and the Herald of Free Enterprise disaster[181], which led to considerable public

---

[178]   [2007] All ER (D) 173 (Jul)
[179]   [2008] All ER (D) 173 (Jul)
[180]   See *R v Balfour Beatty Rail Infrastructure Services Ltd* [2006] EWCA Crim 1586
[181]   See *R. v P & O European Ferries (Dover) Ltd* [1991] 93 Cr. App. R. 72

outcry and to concerns that the criminal law in this area had become outdated.

6.48   As regards individuals however, the common law offence of Gross Negligence Manslaughter still exists and applies to individuals. A duty must be owed by the defendant to the deceased (as is the case with a director to an employee), this duty must have been breached and the question then becomes whether the defendant's conduct fell so far below the standard to be expected that it should be judged criminal.

6.49   An example of the required level of neglect is demonstrated by *R v Adomako (John Asare)*[182] in which an anaesthetist failed to recognise that the tube supplying the patient with oxygen had become disconnected, it remained disconnected until the patient's death approximately 9 minutes later despite the patient's blood pressure dropping. The question is one of fact for a jury to determine, thus the standard will depend on the ordinary person's assessment of what amounts to a criminally negligent breach. The maximum penalty is life imprisonment and the commission of this offence is of particular concern to "hands on" directors as in *The Attorney General's Reference No. 89 of 2006 R v Shaw*[183], due to the greater ease of proving knowledge of the circumstances and of demonstrating a breach of duty.

Directors

6.50   Recent prosecutions appear to indicate that the definition of a director can extend to include a shadow director (a non-director who issues instructions to the directors); and that the definition of an officer can include external consultants, particularly where they are negligent in advising. It should be noted, however, that the definition of manager is designed to catch those with real responsibility and power and

---

[182] [1995] 1 A.C. 171
[183] [2006] All ER (D) 45 (Oct)

therefore is unlikely to catch lower level managers (see *R v Boal*[184]).

6.51   In practice this places an additional layer of legal responsibility on directors, managers and officers, and is indicative of the need for them to take a proactive approach to monitoring health and safety to satisfy themselves that it is being properly considered.

6.52   In the event of a fatality or serious accident, directors, senior managers and officers are almost always firmly in the spotlight, and indeed a critical element of the Corporate Manslaughter offence is the existence of "senior management failings" (discussed further at *Corporate Manslaughter paras 6.131 - 6.136*), in such a way that alternative offences contrary to HASWA can be brought alongside a corporate manslaughter prosecution. Thus, potentially, section 37 prosecutions, a HASWA prosecution of the company and a Corporate Manslaughter Act prosecution could all be brought conjointly against multiple defendants including the senior management.

6.53   In this regard, in view of the potential personal liabilities of individual directors or officers, there is an even greater onus upon directors and senior managers when it comes to health and safety responsibilities. The need not to under-estimate the importance of good systems and procedures in place, training directors and officers on their health and safety responsibilities and taking a positive stance to managing health and safety is more significant when considered below, in relation to the Court's new sentencing powers under the Health and Safety Offences Act 2008[185] and the power to imprison directors.

---

[184] [1992] QB 591
[185] See *Health and Safety Offences Act* below (paras 6.152 – 6.153)

Guidance for Directors' Duties

6.54   In 2001 the Health and Safety Commission issued *"Directors' responsibilities for health and safety"* as a guidance document to help directors to ensure that health and safety risks arising from their organisation's activities are properly managed and that adequate measures are taken to protect both employees and members of the public. The intention is to ensure that the board of directors accept joint responsibility and lead their organisation's health and safety performance. For example, by requiring that the company has:

- a clear health and safety policy and should appoint at least one board member to champion health and safety issues
- ensured that the individual members of the board recognise their personal liabilities and responsibilities under health and safety legislation
- ensured that all board decisions reflect the organisation's health and safety policy

6.55   These considerations apply when making decisions such as how to invest in new equipment, premises and products.

6.56   The Code also advocates companies consulting staff fully on all health and safety issues and that the board of directors be kept informed about health and safety issues affecting the organisation and its performance. Whilst the HSC guidance is not compulsory for directors, following the Code would amount to good evidence of a positive health and safety culture and that they are in compliance with the law.

6.57   The most significant guidance is that issued by the Institute of Directors entitled *"Leading Health and Safety at Work, Actions and Good Practice for Board Members"*. The Code Encourages three essential principles which are:

1.   Strong and active leadership from the top; a visible active commitment from the board; and clear communication throughout the organisation to ensure the integration of good health and safety management with business decisions.

2.   Worker involvement and encouragement of directors to engage the workforce in promoting and achieving safe and healthy conditions and the establishment of effective communication systems and management structures.

3.   Ongoing assessment and review by identifying and managing health and safety risks; encouraging businesses to seek guidance from competent advisors and implement systems for monitoring, reporting and reviewing health and safety performance.

6.58   These two guidance documents give indispensable assistance in establishing a framework for board-led health and safety management within a business.

6.59   Perhaps more significantly is that the guidance has been issued jointly with the Health and Safety Commission. Under the Corporate Manslaughter Act S8(3)(b) a jury can have regard to relevant health and safety guidance. The guidance explicitly states that it is to be classed as "relevant" for the purposes of the Act. Whilst the guidance in itself is not obligatory, if it is followed it is strongly indicative of compliance with health and safety obligations and the absence of a "gross breach" and would allow for a robust defence.

The Reverse Burden of Proof – Reasonable Practicability

6.60   It will be appreciated from initial reading that health and safety obligations are potentially far reaching and onerous, and for this reason it is important to appreciate the interpretation placed upon 'reasonable practicability' by the courts.

6.61   The case of *Tesco Supermarkets Ltd v Nattrass*[186] allowed Tesco to establish a defence under the Trade Descriptions Act by having a complex system in place to ensure that offences were not committed. However there was a due diligence defence available under this legislation.

6.62   Health and Safety law has, however, followed a different course. In the case *of R v British Steel*[187] this was cited in support, however the Court determined that reasonable practicability imposed a more stringent test and that there was no due diligence defence under HASWA. The defendants sought to argue that, provided all reasonable practicable measures had been taken at a level of the company's management which could be ascribed the "directing mind and will", or at a suitably senior management level, that this would provide a defence to the obligation under section 3(1) that an employer should:

conduct his undertaking in such a way as to ensure, so far as reasonably practicable, that persons not in his employment who may be affected are not thereby exposed to risks.

6.63   The court determined that such a defence would emasculate the legislation, and that the offence was one of absolute liability subject to the company having taken all reasonably practicable measures.

Employer's Undertaking and Foreseeability of Risk

6.64   Following on from this the case of *R v Associated Octel Co*

---

[186] [1971] 2 All E.R. 127
[187] [1995] 1 W.L.R. 1356

Ltd[188] involved a large chemical plant undertaking its annual shutdown for maintenance. The victim was a contractor's employee who was cleaning a tank using acetone when the bulb of the lamp he was using broke, igniting the acetone and badly burning him. Associated Octel argued that they were not liable as the injury was not caused by how they had conducted their undertaking but rather by the manner in which the contractors had conducted theirs, a practice over which Associated Octel had no control.

6.65 The court held that undertaking could and did extend to include the contractor's works in this case but that this would be a question of fact in each case. The procedures and control exercised were deciding factors and control will certainly be relevant. It is clear that "undertaking" will be given a wide interpretation. Thus it is probable that repair works being carried out on a section of railway track would fall within, whereas the production of sections of track at a third party's premises would not.

6.66 It should be noted that there is no defence available to an employer that the offence was due to the actions of an employee (section 21 of the Management Regulations). In practice an employer will not always be liable where the actions of an employee are so unforeseeable that they could not have been prevented.

6.67 The case *of R v Nelson Group Services (Maintenance) Ltd*[189] involved the fitting of gas appliances, and in doing so, several fittings were conducted in such a way as to expose the occupiers of the properties to risks to their health. The fitters were properly trained; instructed, certificated, and equipped but nevertheless it was accepted that the fittings were left in a state which exposed the occupiers to risk. The issue in the case was whether the risk was sufficient to

---

[188] [1997] IRLR 123
[189] [1998] 4 All ER 331

convict the company of breach of S3(1). The court confirmed that the conduct of the fitters were part of the conduct of the defendant's undertaking, the remaining question was of reasonable practicability. On this point Roch LJ stated that:

The fact that the employee who was carrying out the work...has done the work carelessly or omitted to take a precaution he should have taken does not of itself preclude the employer from establishing that everything that was reasonably practicable in the conduct of the employer's undertaking to ensure that third persons affected by the employer's undertaking were not exposed to risks to their health and safety had been done... it is a sufficient obligation... to protect the public to require the employer to show that everything reasonably practicable has been done to see that a person doing the work has the appropriate skill and instruction.

6.68   Therefore, with suitable and sufficient systems in place to train and supervise employees it is possible to argue that the employer has not exposed a third party to risk. This is borne out by *R v HTM Ltd*[190] in which two employees moved a telescopic tower without lowering it, as they had been trained to do. The tower made contact with an overhead power cable and both were fatally injured. The court confirmed that foreseeability is *"a tool with which to assess the likelihood of a risk eventuating"*. On the facts the accident was entirely attributable to the fault of an employee and the employer could not have foreseen the risk.

6.69   *R v Chargot Ltd*[191] involved the prosecution of the victim's employer (under section 2(1) HASWA) and the chief contractor (under section 3(1) HASWA) following a fatality.

---

[190] [2006] EWCA Crim 1156
[191] [2008] UKHL 73

6.70   On appeal to the House of Lords the court considered the systems of work and recognised that the method of enforcing these systems was by inspection. They also affirmed *R v Board of Trustees of the Science Museum*[192] that the burden of proof lay with the defendant to prove reasonable practicability and that it would suffice for the prosecution to rely on the fact of the accident's occurrence to prove risk.

6.71   However, the court did state that the law does not seek to create a risk free environment, and that the risk must be "material" and one *"which any reasonable person would appreciate and take steps to guard against"*. The Judgment in *Chargot* was considered to formalise a requirement for the prosecution to prove "foreseeability" in order to establish the existence of a risk in Health and Safety prosecutions, an approach which was followed in *HSE v Norwest Holst Limited and Costain Limited*[193].

6.72   This interpretation has been rejected by the Court of Appeal in *R v EGS Ltd*[194]. The court held that foreseeability was relevant as part of the reasonable practicability assessment but that whether a risk was material and foreseeable should be a question of fact, i.e. it did not create an additional hurdle for the prosecution to satisfy when proving risk as *Chargot* seemed to suggest. It is curious that, in spite of this robust and rigid ruling, when the case was retried two of the defendants were nevertheless acquitted by the jury, and this may demonstrate that foreseeability is clearly a matter of subjective perception on the facts of each particular case.

Material Risk

6.73   The case of *R v Porter*[195] related to the death of a young

---

[192]   [1993] 3 All ER 853, [1993] 1 WLR 1171
[193]   2007 WL 4587097
[194]   [2009] EWCA 1942
[195]   [2008] EWCA Crim 1271

child who fell down steps in a playground and later died from MRSA infection in hospital, the Court of Appeal confirmed that a risk, which the prosecution has to prove, must be *"real, as opposed to fanciful or hypothetical"*. Additionally, risk that formed a part of everyday incidents of life went to the issue of whether an injured person was exposed to risk by the "conduct" of the defendant's operation.

6.74　Thus, employers will not be liable for accidents arising out of everyday risks and a robust defence of accidents will often be mounted where accidents arise out of similar facts.

Investigations

6.75　If, in the aftermath of an accident, a risk is established or identified, an inspector will conduct an investigation. This will include gathering evidence, speaking to and taking statements from employees, seizing documents and inspecting premises. This is often an area in which confusion arises as to a defendant's exact rights. Adopting a robust approach at the investigation stage can often significantly impact on the extent of any prosecution that may be brought and in the event of a conviction, the level of any fine. As there are numerous tactical and legal considerations it is essential for a defendant to take advice as soon as possible once an investigation has commenced.

Voluntary Witness Statements

6.76　The usual type of witness statement taken in criminal proceedings (including health and safety) is a voluntary witness statement made under the provisions of Section 9 of the Criminal Justice Act 1967.

6.77　The contents are admissible in Court without the witness attending to give oral evidence. These statements are most commonly used by investigators wishing to record factual circumstances.

6.78   The witness making the voluntary statement is not immune from self-incrimination if anything he says indicates his guilt for an offence. If these events do transpire, the witness statement process should be concluded and the witness re-interviewed under caution.

Compelled Witness Statements under Section 20 of HASWA

6.79   Section 20 of HASWA gives an inspector the power to require any person whom the inspector has reasonable cause to believe will be able to provide information relevant to an examination or investigation, to answer such questions as the inspector thinks fit, and to sign a declaration of the truth of the answers. This power is not exercisable by the police.

6.80   Only the information provided by the witness should be recorded and, therefore, usual practice is to conduct the interview on a question and answer basis.

6.81   Magistrates' Courts can commit health and safety cases to the Crown Court for either trial or sentence in the event they feel their sentencing powers are not sufficient. These are known as committal proceedings. At committal stage, the prosecution must put before the Court sufficient evidence to establish "a case to answer" against the defendant. Section 9 statements are an exception to the general rule relating to hearsay evidence and can be relied on even if the witness is not in attendance. A Section 20 statement however cannot in itself be relied on as evidence and so if these are the principle form of statement utilised, this makes the committal stage a more difficult hurdle for prosecutors to overcome.

6.82   At trial, even if the witness's evidence is not in dispute, the witness will still have to be called to give evidence in person.

6.83   Section 20 also prevents the use of any evidence contained within the statement against the maker of that statement or their spouse.

Workplace Fatalities

6.84   The HSE joint protocol for liaison in relation to work-related deaths requires the police to take the lead in any workplace fatality investigation. They will focus their investigation on corporate manslaughter, which requires evidence of senior management failings. The evidence of senior management practices will be central to the investigation and an organisational structure management chart will normally be requested.

6.85   In the early stages of an investigation the police will conduct the vast majority of interviews, often, but not always, accompanied by inspectors. The police cannot compel witnesses to either give or sign a Section 9 statement, although the attendance of witnesses can be ensured through the service of a witness summons to compel attendance at court. It is good practice, in the event of a fatality, to have legal representatives attend site from the outset and to take statements from the relevant employees to prepare the internal accident investigation report. Representatives should also act as a point of contact to arrange any witness interviews which the police request. If possible, employees should be interviewed by employers for accident investigation before they give a statement to the police.

Obtaining Copies of Statements

6.86   Many witnesses wish to retain a copy of their statement. The strict legal position is that if a witness requests a copy, then a copy should be provided. However, inspectors and the police do have a wide discretion to refuse to provide a copy, if the provision of a statement to a witness would be likely to interfere with the course of justice. Home Office advice suggests that such situations might arise where the statement is sought to enable the witness to lie consistently or where others are bringing pressure on the witness to obtain a copy of the statement with a view to persuading the individual to change what they have said. It could however potentially include situations where the inspector genuinely believes that a witness may compare his or her statement with those of others, including the employer's legal representatives.

6.87   Practical experience suggests that whilst a witness can request a copy of his or her statement, police and inspectors often exercise this discretion to prevent copies being circulated to the company's legal representatives.

6.88   Ordinarily, witness statements are only served on the defence if they are to be relied on in criminal proceedings.

Legal Representation Whilst Providing Statements

6.89   As a matter of law, a witness is not entitled to have a legal advisor present whilst providing a voluntary statement. A witness can however request the presence of a representative, which can include a solicitor. This person could also be a representative from his employer. Interviewers can exercise their discretion as to whether to allow this person to attend and/or take notes at the interview.

6.90   In relation to Section 20 statements, the giver has a statutory right to have any person present whilst making it. This is caveated by a requirement for the inspector's approval although in practice this is rarely refused. This can include a solicitor, trade union representative or friend. For witnesses, a Section 20 statement is therefore usually in their best interests and therefore generally to be preferred.

6.91   For either form of statement, the person providing the statement is usually represented by an independent solicitor acting solely in their interests and who is usually recommended by the solicitors acting for the employer and/or insurers.

6.92   The advantage of this is that the solicitor who is present can take a contemporaneous note of the statement given by the employee and, with the consent of the individual employee, can discuss or even disclose the content of that statement to employers or legal representatives.

6.93   Irrespective of whether a witness is providing a voluntary Section 9 statement or a compelled Section 20 statement, there is clear Law Society Guidance for solicitors stating that a solicitor acting for the employer should not represent an employee giving a statement if there is a conflict of interest or a significant risk of such a conflict between them. Conflicts of interest usually arise in such cases and the employer's solicitors should usually not accompany employees whilst they provide a witness statement.

6.94   The choice of whether to give a voluntary Section 9 witness statement or not is entirely the employee's and the employer should not attempt to influence this decision. However it is advisable for an employee to be informed of the benefits of providing a Section 20 compelled statement, namely the inability of the prosecutor to use evidence so obtained against the maker.

6.95   An employee can refuse to make a Section 9 statement by either refusing to attend a voluntary witness statement interview or attending and insisting that the interview take place as a compelled Section 20 statement, thereby forcing the inspector's process.

6.96   Both employees and employers benefit from the use of Section 20 statements due to the statutory protection against self-incrimination, their inadmissibility in committal proceedings and the prospect of having an independent adviser in attendance to record what is said.

Police and Inspector Powers - Investigations and Site Visits Following An Accident

6.97   Police will investigate in cases involving a workplace and will liaise with the regulator throughout their involvement.

6.98   Employers often find police involvement in the investigation to be challenging, as the police will employ their standard procedures in relation to a crime scene which is often burdensome in a workplace e.g. they may want to set up an incident room and will employ a "door to door" method of investigation which will usually involve interviewing everyone from station personnel to senior management. It is normally wise to co-operate as fully as possible so as not to obstruct a criminal investigation or the conduct of a police officer's duties.

6.99   The police and inspectors have a statutory right to enter the workplace. In practice all work activity will stop and the relevant areas of the workplace will be cordoned off. The employer should take steps to secure the scene as far as possible and make it safe immediately after an accident. It is important not to remove any plant or machinery, or do anything to clean or cover up the scene. This could potentially lead to an investigation for perverting the course of justice, which carries a greater sentence that any health and safety offence.

6.100   The police and inspectors both have powers to seize and retain equipment connected to the accident. Normal practice is to undertake a joint accident reconstruction and retain any pieces of equipment for any further examination or testing that may be necessary as it may provide potential evidence in a prosecution. The police have a duty to retain criminal evidence until the conclusion of any prosecution. Even where it is not the direct cause, best practice is to retain relevant equipment until the investigation is concluded.

6.101 The police and inspectors can also seize documents they consider relevant to their investigation, usually including risk assessments, method statements, inspection and training records etc. It is good practice in the aftermath of an accident to copy all documents so that these can be provided without losing possession of key evidence.

Privilege and Internal Investigations

6.102 Certain documents, those created with the dominant purpose of actual or contemplated litigation, or for the giving or receiving of legal advice, may be legally privileged. These documents should be marked "covered by legal privilege" and should not be seized. In practice these documents are sometimes seized with their status falling 'to be determined later'. If such documents are seized legal advice should be sought and detailed notes retained. In the event any such evidence being relied on, legal arguments will then determine whether it should be excluded.

6.103 It is suggested that best practice is to begin an internal investigation immediately, to establish what happened and highlight improvements to be made to working practices. There is a developing jurisprudence over whether such reports can be privileged but it is good practice to take legal advice upon and communicate the investigation to solicitors to assist in asserting legal privilege later. Failure to do so can lead to a report containing damaging conclusions being disclosable to the prosecution. The report should be limited to a few key individuals. If a copy of the report is requested employers should take legal advice before acceding. As part of this process, a specific point of contact should be established to deal with the internal investigation and liaise with regulatory bodies and legal advisers.

Interviews under Caution

6.104 Once an investigation is concluded the inspectors may have evidence of breaches of the legislation or a suspicion that offences have been committed and will want to put questions to the potential defendant at an interview under caution.

6.105   The "right to silence" stems from the basic common law right against self-incrimination and the principle that everyone is innocent until proven guilty and for natural persons is protected by the Human Rights Act 1998.

6.106   This right is reflected in the caution given when questioning suspects. These provisions are contained within Code C of the Code of Practice to the Police and Criminal Evidence Act 1984 ("PACE").

6.107   Under the Code of Practice to PACE the investigating officer must set out the reasonable objective grounds for suspicion which have led to the request for an interview under caution; must confirm the offence(s) under investigation or which it is suspected that the person may have committed; and must confirm what evidence suggests that the offence has been committed and that the person to be questioned committed it.

6.108   Furthermore, a person who is a suspect of an offence must be cautioned before any questions (or further questions, if answers to previous questions have given grounds for the suspicion) are put to him for the purpose of obtaining evidence which may be given in a prosecution. In the absence of a caution the court has the discretion to exclude any evidence given by that person.

6.109   Health and safety offences are not arrestable (for corporate offenders, individuals can now be arrested under the Health and Safety Offences Act, see paras 6.147 – 6.151), and therefore a written invitation is usually sent requesting attendance for an interview under caution. Upon receipt of such a request there are numerous tactical and legal considerations and it is best practice to obtain legal advice due to the developing jurisprudence and widely differing potential circumstances.

6.110 It is often advisable to request confirmation of the suspected offence and the reasonable grounds for suspicion, as this prevents such interviews being employed as information gathering exercises.

6.111 It should be noted that factual considerations, such as a person's role within an organisation, do not automatically provide an objective ground for reasonable suspicion of an offence and best practice is therefore to request this information, to which the interviewee is entitled, to justify the request.

6.112 Whilst the interview under caution is the inspector's chance to confirm the existence of a breach, it also presents the defence with an opportunity to demonstrate the reasonably practicable measures in place to control risk in order to lay the foundations for a later defence. Alternatively it provides an opportunity to plead guilty at the first opportunity and put forward the points to be raised in mitigation of the offence.

Enforcement

6.113 The powers of an inspector are not simply limited to bringing a prosecution, indeed the regime in place would be considered draconian if they were. In order to cater to the varying ranges of breach there are other options available short of instigating a prosecution.

6.114 As in all cases inspectors may give informal guidance or direction. HSE guidance on the topic states that inspectors should provide written copies of their advice on request and should clarify the difference between legal requirements and best practice.

Enforcement Notices

6.115 Often investigation is accompanied by service of Improvement or Prohibition Notices if the inspector considers that there is a serious risk of personal injury or a potential breach of health and safety legislation. Although serious, a notice does not, however, rule out a prosecution. Non-compliance is very serious and could result in prosecution of the company and any individual responsible for the breach, with the potential for imprisonment of the latter.

6.116   An employer disputing a notice should seek legal advice as compliance is a double-edged sword. Whilst non-compliance is an offence, compliance is often illustrative of further reasonably practicable measures that could have been taken and is an implicit acknowledgement of breaches.

Improvement Notices

6.117   Where an inspector is of the opinion that an employer is contravening, has contravened, or is likely to contravene, any of the statutory health and safety provisions he may serve an Improvement Notice which requires compliance by the employer to remedy a breach within a minimum of 21 days. Further enforcement can, and usually will, follow should the employer fail to comply.

Prohibition Notices

6.118   In cases where an inspector is of the opinion that an activity gives or will give rise to a risk of serious personal injury, an inspector may serve a prohibition notice which requires the activity giving rise to the risk to cease either immediately, or after a specified period, until the breach is remedied. In practice, following a serious workplace injury such a notice is invariably issued to prevent recurrence.

6.119   Failure to comply with either form of notice is a serious offence and gives rise to a potential fine of £20,000 and six months imprisonment in a magistrates' court or an unlimited fine in the crown court.

Notices and Appeals

6.120   Appeals against either type of notice can be made within 21 days from the date of service (or longer, if more time is given) to an Employment Tribunal. Failure to do so will mean that the employer acquiesces to the terms of the notice; this will have a detrimental effect on the employer's health and safety record.

6.121   An example of a successful challenge comes from the case of *Chilcott v Thermal Transfer Ltd*[196] in which an employee fell from a working platform and suffered injury. A HSE inspector was inspecting the site and was informed of the accident. The Tribunal's decision was appealed to the High Court which stated that the question to be asked is whether *"they, if they had been in the position of the Inspector, would have served that notice."* On the facts, as a suitable and sufficient working plan was in place, the Notice was cancelled. Appeals will therefore look at issues such as: whether it is reasonably practicable to comply; whether service of the notice is a proper and proportionate use of an enforcement power; and whether the requirements of the notice were clear, free from confusion, or if the notice was flawed (i.e. if the wrong legislation is referred to).

6.122   It should however be noted with caution that an employment tribunal can substitute new wording to a notice on appeal, thus they will look broadly at whether a notice was merited and may substitute new words so as to correct the notice.

6.123   If an Enforcement Notice is served, it should not be taken lightly as it can have a detrimental effect on a company's health and safety record and a significant impact on other commercial concerns for a business, such as insurance premiums or tendering prospects. A notice remains on the

---

[196] [2009] EWHC 2086 (Admin)

register for 5 years and can be used as evidence of bad character in the event of future prosecutions.

Cautions

6.124 Simple Cautions (formerly known as Formal Cautions) can be employed by an inspector where an offence has been committed and the employer accepts this but deems that prosecution is not appropriate.

6.125 Guidance states that a Simple Caution should never be issued where the accused disputes liability for the offence. In practice, many employers accept them for commercial reasons to avoid protracted litigation over minor or technical infractions.

6.126 Some regulators are willing to accept Cautions in lieu of prosecution for minor infractions, as it is often a proportionate method of dealing with a breach, the caution remaining on the employer's record providing evidence of bad character in future prosecutions.

Enforcement Policy

6.127 The ORR's enforcement policy is "consistent with that issued by the HSC to the HSE and local authorities" (ORR Enforcement Policy Statement). The broad principles applied when assessing which method of enforcement to adopt are:

Proportionality	Taking action which is appropriate to the risk;
Targeting	Ensuring that those responsible for creating the most serious risks are prosecuted;
Consistency	Ensuring that similar results result from similar circumstances;

Transparency   Telling employers what is and isn't
                  expected of them;

Accountability   Acting in accordance with the policies
                  and guidance laid down by the ORR.

6.128   The determination of whether to prosecute is made by the application of a twofold test, namely the evidential and public interest tests. The evidential test requires the prosecutor to believe that there is sufficient evidence to secure a reasonable prospect of conviction, the public interest test is designed to determine whether there are public interest factors that weigh against the presumption of prosecuting where there is sufficient evidence to do so.

6.129   The Code recognises that, the more serious the offence, the more likely that a prosecution will be in the public interest, thus in the aftermath of a workplace death or serious injury, a prosecution occurs in the vast majority of cases.

6.130   Making representations to a regulator within the framework of its enforcement policy often has merit in relation to less serious breaches and can often dissuade the regulator from prosecuting.

Corporate Manslaughter

6.131   Perhaps the most significant development in the past two years was the enactment of the Corporate Manslaughter Act and Corporate Homicide 2008. The Act put corporate killing on a statutory footing for the first time, creating the offence of "corporate manslaughter" for organisations if the way in which their activities were managed or organised:

(a)   causes a person's death; and
(b)   amounts to a gross breach of a relevant duty of care owed by the organisation to the deceased.

6.132   An organisation is guilty of an offence only if the way in which its activities are managed or organised by its senior management is a substantial element in the breach.

6.133   The main emphasis of the Act is on failings by the "senior management" of an organisation in relation to how activities are managed or organised. Thus, those whose role is decisive or influential at a national, divisional or regional level are likely to have their decisions closely examined. This will therefore cover board level policy and procedure, as well as operational implementation.

6.134   For liability to be established there must be a gross breach of a duty of care owed by the organisation to the deceased, which has caused the death (section 1). The relevant duties of care are defined under section 2 and include Occupier's and Employer's duties such as those of employer to employee under HASWA.

6.135   As mentioned previously the factors for the jury to consider (under section 8) include seriousness or risk, and the regard paid to relevant guidance.

6.136   The definition of senior management is wide and could conceivably include individual site managers or project managers, depending on the remit of their role. It seems likely that such a prosecution will go hand in hand with the prosecution of senior management for gross negligence manslaughter or section 37 HASWA, as much of the evidence of one defendant will tend to incriminate the other[197]. For this reason, where there is the potential for such an investigation, senior management and the company must have separate representation due to the high likelihood of a conflict of interests arising. Proposed sentencing for corporate manslaughter is discussed further below.

---

[197] see previous discussion in *Health and Safety Corporate Liability,* paras 6.30 – 6.35

Prosecutions in the Rail Sector

6.137 Hatfield, Potters Bar, Selby, Paddington, and more recently Tebay and Ufton Nervet have all left impressions emblazoned on the public consciousness.

6.138 All but Tebay involved derailments and all led to multiple fatalities. The rail sector has come under increasing scrutiny and regulators have come under increasing pressure to ensure that such incidents do not occur.

6.139 Fining trends are discussed in more detail below but the figures for rail prosecutions speak for themselves. Following Paddington, Network Rail received a £4m fine whilst Thames Trains were fined £2m. After Hatfield, Balfour Beatty and Railtrack received fines of £7.5m and £3.5m respectively. Accidents which expose the public to risk, particularly where this leads to multiple deaths and/or serious injuries have historically attracted the largest fines. The rail sector is by its nature exposed to such risks, as a single derailment or collision could potentially lead to hundreds of deaths that would certainly, in line with current trends, lead to a fine of millions of pounds.

6.140 Nor are the consequences purely monetary. Following Tebay the head of MAC Machinery Services and a crane operative were sentenced to prison terms of nine years (reduced on appeal to seven) and two years respectively for manslaughter by gross negligence.

6.141 There has not been an incident of this nature in the rail sector for over five years but the ORR record of prosecutions, prohibition and improvement notices still demonstrate that there are major concerns. This extends to all activities involving trains, and major areas of concern remain electrocution, derailment, mobile elevated working platforms ("MEWP"), train collisions (with vehicles and pedestrians), work at height, level crossings, and signals passed at danger.

6.142   These issues do not simply extend to Network Rail but include TOCs, contractors, and members of the public (it should be remembered that Gary Hart, whose vehicle was responsible for the Selby rail crash was sentenced to five years in prison for causing death by dangerous driving).

6.143   The highest fines recorded in recent years relate to:

- electrocution, which has attracted fines of £200,000 where severe burns were suffered by an injured employee;
- derailment, where fines as high as £275,000 have been imposed despite the absence of any fatalities or severe injuries;
- MEWP usage, leading to a fine of £240,000 where defects have resulted in a fatality;
- an individual being struck by a train, leading to a £130,000 fine for Network Rail. The contractor responsible was also fined £33,000 where a track worker was struck by a train.

6.144   It is clear that the approach adopted is not only based on the actual consequences of a breach but also on the potential consequences. A single derailment, for instance, may result in no serious injuries but represents the potential for a multiple fatality incident and, as such, the fines attracted are high.

6.145   A useful demonstration of this point can be derived from the case of *R v Jarvis Facilities Ltd*[198] in which a fine of £400,000 was initially imposed for a derailment involving no serious injuries, resulting from defective track maintenance works. The responsible contractor appealed and succeeded in reducing the fine to £275,000 with the Court of Appeal identifying that the Judge was entitled to take account of public outrage and a legitimate element of deterrence.

---

[198] [2005] EWCA Crim 1409

6.146   The rail industry is generally a high risk, high profile and high turnover industry; this perception and associated public outcry would be reflected in the level of fine imposed in the aftermath of a major accident.

Health and Safety Sentences, Fines and General Trends

Health and Safety Offences Act

6.147   The most significant development in sentencing came in January 2009 when the Health and Safety Offences Act 2008 came into force. The legislation is designed to provide more powerful deterrents to health and safety offences. The Act increases maximum fines in the Magistrates' Courts from £5,000 to £20,000 for breaches of the Regulations. It makes certain offences which were previously only triable in a Magistrates' Court triable in the Crown Court and, perhaps most worryingly for individuals, the power to impose terms of imprisonment of up to 2 years for convictions in the Crown Court (or up to 12 months for cases in the Magistrates' Court).

6.148   As well as applying to, amongst others, the general duties under Sections 2 and 3 of the Health and Safety at Work Act, the new powers also apply to offences under Sections 7 and 37.

6.149   As yet there have been no reported imprisonments of an individual using the new sentencing powers, but it is only a matter of time as, prior to the new enactment, fines for individuals and individual prosecutions became increasingly severe. Such fines have the potential to lead to a term of imprisonment, as failure to pay a fine is a contempt of Court.

6.150   In addition to the threat of imprisonment the Company Director Disqualification Act 1986 allows a sentencing court to make a Disqualification Order against a person convicted of an offence in connection with the management of a company. This would prevent that individual from acting as a director, liquidator, receiver, manager or in any way being involved with the promotion, formation or management of a company for a fixed period of up to 5 years, if convicted in the Magistrates' Court, and up to 15 years if convicted in the Crown Court.

6.151 This is potentially the area of Health and Safety law where the most significant developments and challenges are likely to come about in the near future. For instance, an individual convicted and imprisoned may seek to challenge the reverse burden of proof and the absence of any requirement for intent by reference to the Human Rights Act 1998, with the potential to take a case to the European Court of Human Rights. It is perhaps anomalous that an alleged murderer or war criminal should face greater protection under the law than a company director because of the nature of the reverse burden when compared to the requirement for 'beyond reasonable doubt' in criminal law.

Corporate Manslaughter and Corporate Homicide Act 2008

6.152 The Corporate Manslaughter and Corporate Homicide Act 2008 provides that an unlimited fine can be imposed in the event of a conviction. In calculating penalties, courts currently examine the pre and post tax profits of a corporate defendant to determine a reasonable fine.

6.153 In November 2007 the Sentencing Advisory Panel recommended that turnover should be used instead for convictions under the new Corporate Manslaughter Act. They suggested that penalties should be between 2.5% and 10% of turnover, which would mean that a business with a turnover of £1 billion, minimum fines of £25m would have been imposed. The Advisory panel further recommended that a prosecution involving a fatality under other health and safety legislation should result in a fine of between 1% and 7% of turnover.

6.154   This approach was not adopted by the Sentencing Guidelines Council on 27 October 2009 who proposed that corporate manslaughter fines should be measured in the millions of pounds and should rarely fall below £500,000. They also indicated that for health and safety offences causing death, fines should seldom be lower than £100,000.

6.155   The Corporate Manslaughter and Corporate Homicide Act 2008 also provides additional sentencing options, such as a Remedial Order requiring correction of the identified health and safety failings and, perhaps most powerfully, a Publicity Order which will force a business to publicise the conviction which is likely to hugely damage its reputation.

6.156   At the time of writing it is anticipated that the first corporate manslaughter trial, of Cotswold Geotechnical Holdings Limited, will take place on 23 February 2010 at Bristol Crown Court. The trial is expected to last approximately 6 weeks and it will be watched with great interest in terms of the legal issues that are heard, as well as the sentences that will be imposed in the event of a conviction, utilising the new sentencing powers under the legislation.

6.157   Whilst it is always difficult to accurately identify trends in sentencing, fines of £100,000 are now likely to be standard for cases involving fatalities, even those involving small to medium enterprises. Indeed in some recent cases, the courts have not been afraid to impose levels of fines which have equalled or exceeded the previous year's profits.

6.158   Rail prosecutions appear to be broadly comparable to the present trends in health and safety regulation. Some of the highest levels of fines recorded in the last two years are cases involving fatalities such as *R v FJ Chalcroft*[199] and *R v TDG*[200][201] which attracted fines of £260,000 and £275,000

---

[199] [2008] EWCA Crim 770
[200] EWCA Crim 1963

respectively and *R v Bodycote HIP*[202] *Ltd.*, where a double fatality attracted an exceptional fine of £533,000.

6.159   For fatalities, a range of £150,000 to £200,000 for companies, which are capable of surviving such a fine and which cannot be shown to have knowingly "put profits before safety", is a broadly accurate guideline in such prosecutions. Prosecution costs have usually ranged from £20,000 to £100,000 although in exceptional cases prosecution costs have exceeded the fine, and this is particularly the case where appeals are made or a range of experts or multiple defendants are involved.

6.160   The potential still exists for fines to vastly exceed the normal scope, as they did in the aftermath of Hatfield and Paddington. The prosecution of Transco PLC in Scotland for an explosion due to defective gas pipes which caused the deaths of a family of 4 led to a fine of £15m for breach of section 3 of HASWA. The potential for public harm can also be seen in the £1m total fine imposed on Cadbury's for the now notorious Salmonella outbreak in early 2006, and whilst this was imposed for food hygiene offences, it is a useful demonstration that the potential for harm heavily influences the level of fine imposed. This is clearly analogous to the rail sector where there is often a potential for wide ranging harm combined with a high public profile. The case of *London Fire & Emergency Planning Authority v Shell*[203] is a further good example of this. A fine of £300,000 was imposed for breaches of fire safety at one of Shell's sites even though there was no major incident and no injuries resulted. This demonstrates that the potential for harm is often a major factor in cases where fines are being considered.

6.161   The courts have identified that fines are designed to make

---

[201]   [2008]
[202]   Unreported
[203]   Unreported

clear to corporations and their shareholders that they must ensure safety for workers and the general public whilst not pushing businesses into insolvency and thereby punishing the workforce.

Aggravating and Mitigating Factors

6.162   The relevant factors taken into consideration were identified by the Court of Appeal in the leading case on the topic, *R v F Howe and Son Engineers Ltd*[204] and include:

- *how far short of the appropriate standard the defendant fell in failing to meet the reasonably practicable test* (thus, if a defendant fails to establish that a risk was not "material", he will nevertheless be in a good position to mitigate a resultant fine);
- *the degree of risk and extent of the danger created by the offence;*
- *the extent of the breach or breaches...whether it was an isolated incident or continued over a period;*
- *the defendant's resources and the effect of the fine on its business.* Although, in practice, it may determine the scope of a defendant's resources and the probable effect of a fine, the size of the business is not a factor when sentencing, as the duty of care remains identical and *the standard of care imposed by the legislation is the same regardless of the size of the company.* This applies to both corporate and individual offenders.

6.163   Aggravating features, that will lead to a larger fine, include:

- Generally, in circumstances where "death or serious injury" results, it is regarded as an aggravating feature of the offence. The penalty should reflect public disquiet at the unnecessary loss of life.

---

[204] [1999] 2 All ER 249

- Where the defendant has deliberately profited financially from a failure to take necessary health and safety steps or specifically "run a risk to save money" this "seriously aggravates the offence.
- "A failure to heed warnings", thus a failure to take notice of guidance or to recognise the existence of a risk, will increase the level of fine received.

6.164   Mitigating features, that will reduce the fine, include:

- A "prompt admission of responsibility and a timely plea of guilty". It should be noted that a first instance guilty plea to any offence will generally attract a reduction in the resulting fine of one third. It should however be borne in mind that, in the Crown Court, fines are unlimited and there are no rigid rules on sentencing.
- "Steps to remedy deficiencies after they are drawn to the defendant's attention". This can be seen as avoiding double punishment, so as not to discourage defendants from being proactive in the aftermath of an accident.
- "a good safety record". The Inspectorate, as a matter of course, will examine the defendant's record for evidence of bad character and previous convictions and will draw these to the attention of the court. Similarly, it is good practice on the part of the defence to draw good character and existing healthy and safety measures to the court's attention.

6.165   The ideal time for a defendant to raise such points is at an interview under caution, which provides an opportunity for the defendant to present such considerations in an appropriate forum.

6.166   A defendant will be given an overview of what the prosecution consider to be the key facts and aggravating features of a case. This approach derives from the case of *R v Friskies Petcare UK Ltd*[205] and gives the defendant vital information about the presentation and tone of the prosecution. This "Friskies schedule" will be served at the commencement of proceedings and the defendant, if pleading guilty, will serve a responding document setting out the mitigating factors to be taken into account. Often the schedule serves as the basis of any agreement between the parties as to a basis of plea and such an agreed basis should be recorded and filed with the court.

6.167 In assessing the means of the defendant, the starting point for a corporate defendant will be the annual accounts. These will be supplied to the court so that an assessment of means can be made if the defendant wishes to address the court on its ability to pay.

Defence Costs

6.168 The Treasury recently introduced changes to cap defence costs for privately funded defendants in the event of a successful defence. Defendants can no longer reclaim defence costs beyond legal aid rates. The prospect arises of an increase in insurance premiums providing legal expense cover or guilty pleas to charges which would otherwise have been defended.

Case Management Between Company and insurer

6.169 From a case management perspective a common approach should be taken to defending both criminal prosecutions and resultant civil actions for personal injury. Often there are conflicting objectives as, for public policy reasons, insurers cannot pay criminal fines on behalf of a company.

---

[205] [2000] 2 Cr App Rep (S) 401, CA

6.170   Thus, an insurer's short-term interest may be best served by encouraging an early guilty plea by the company to keep costs low, whilst a company, understandably, will wish to contest or mitigate the offence as far as they are able. The conflict can be reconciled to some extent where there is an intimated civil action; conviction for a health and safety offence is very strong, de facto evidence of negligence. Thus, an insurer wishing to take a longer-term view may wish to invest resources in contesting a prosecution on behalf of the insured and/or to agree an appropriate basis of plea.

6.171   It is also worth remembering that events such as the Coroner's Inquest will be relevant to both the civil and criminal cases and this means that an effective use of resources will include encouragement of collaboration and sharing of information between the criminal and civil defence legal advisers.

6.172   Evidence disclosed during criminal proceedings may assist the civil case. For example, it may be challenged or discredited. Evidence obtained to prepare a defence is also often useful. For instance, if evidence, or the viewpoint of an expert, is obtained in the criminal case which points to civil liability, this can be disclosed early to the insurers so as to allow an early settlement. This may prevent the unnecessary expenditure of costs in a futile defence.

6.173   There is also a considerable overlap in concepts such as foreseeability, contributory negligence (which may give rise to question of third party act or default), and duties of care. Additionally, expert evidence, which deals with issues of causation, is likely to be produced in both sets of proceedings. A view can be taken in civil proceedings based on the findings in the criminal court.

Guidance to an Employer Following an Accident

6.174 It cannot be overemphasised how much the actions in the immediate aftermath of an accident in relation to an investigation will impact upon the course of events and the eventual outcome.

6.175 Isolate any sources of danger by, if necessary, turning off machinery, isolating power sources, and cease the work activity which led to the accident.

6.176 Where appropriate (where the injured party is an employee or the party was in control of the premises), a RIDDOR report should be made and a record retained.

6.177 An injured party's family should be contacted and compassionate leave or counselling offered to employees if appropriate.

6.178 Cordon off the accident scene. Do not clean it up as this could be construed as tampering.

6.179 Appoint a central point of contact to deal with information requests from the authorities and media, and inform all employees of this person's identity.

6.180 A press release should be drafted in preparation for any media interest. In the event of a fatality, the legal adviser will go on record with the coroner as an interested party in anticipation of the inquest.

6.181 Specialist legal advice should be sought for issues regarding interviews and privilege.

6.182 Conduct an internal accident investigation in the light of legal advice and guidance and alert the insurers of the accident, taking multiple copies of documents so that copies can be provided to the authorities.

6.183 Co-operate with and allow access to the Police and Inspectors, obtaining advice as to the status of documents before disclosing them, any that are privileged should be marked as such and separately stored, and retain records and equipment until the investigation is concluded.

6.184 Legal advice should then be sought in regard to witness interviews, employee representation, whether to appeal or comply with any Enforcement notice, going on record as an interested party to any inquest, and attendance of interviews under caution.

Guidance for Claims' Managers

6.185 Ensure that legal representatives provide full and regular updates which may assist in settling any civil claim.

6.186 Offer to pay for independent representation for employees at interviews under caution or the voluntary provision of statements as this will be beneficial in assessing the course of the investigation and prevent inadvertent or deliberate incrimination of the employer by ensuring that the "community of interests" is preserved.

6.187 Assess the type of insurance possessed by the client, Directors' and Officers' policies in particular usually contemplate such proceedings.

6.188 Bring this note to the insured's attention to allow them to avoid costly errors at the outset of the matter.

INDEX

(References are to paragraph numbers)